The *Leadership in Action* Series

ON LEADING
THE GLOBAL
ORGANIZATION

Center for Creative Leadership

www.ccl.org

The Center for Creative Leadership is an international, nonprofit educational institution founded in 1970 to advance the understanding, practice, and development of leadership for the benefit of society worldwide. As a part of this mission, it publishes books and reports that aim to contribute to a general process of inquiry and understanding in which ideas related to leadership are raised, exchanged, and evaluated. The ideas presented in its publications are those of the author or authors.

The Center thanks you for supporting its work through the purchase of this volume. If you have comments, suggestions, or questions about any CCL Press publications, please contact the Director of Publications at the address given below.

Center for Creative Leadership
Post Office Box 26300
Greensboro, North Carolina 27438-6300
Telephone 336 288 7210
www.ccl.org

Stephen Rush, Editor

With an Introduction by Kelly M. Hannum

The *Leadership in Action* Series

ON LEADING THE GLOBAL ORGANIZATION

CENTER FOR CREATIVE LEADERSHIP
Greensboro, North Carolina

CCL Stock Number 199
©2013 Center for Creative Leadership

Published by CCL Press
Sylvester Taylor, Director of Assessments, Tools, and Publications
Peter Scisco, Manager, Publication Development
Stephen Rush, Editor
Karen Lewis, Editor
Shaun Martin, Associate Editor

Design and layout by Joanne Ferguson

Library of Congress Cataloging-in-Publication Data
On leading the global organization / Stephen Rush, editor ; with an Introduction by Kelly M. Hannum.
    pages cm. — (The leadership in action series)
  Includes bibliographical references and index.
  ISBN 978-1-60491-164-0 (print on demand : alk. paper) — ISBN 978-1-60491-165-7 (e-book) 1. Leadership—Cross-cultural studies.
2. Management—Cross-cultural studies. 3. International business enterprises—Management. I. Rush, Stephen, 1954-

  HD57.7.O474 2013
  658.4'092—dc23

                                                                2013026499

CONTENTS

IN BRIEF

Managers who transition to global leadership roles after previously serving in a mostly domestic capacity quickly learn that there is a world of difference between the two. Many find that their skills don't match the requirements of their new assignments and that they must develop new, expanded, and more diverse and complex skills in order to excel in a global context. The pieces in this book will help global leaders—whether experienced or new to the role—hone or acquire the abilities and behaviors needed to succeed in managing a global operation. Readers will come away with newly formed knowledge on issues related to global leadership and newly formed thoughts on how to successfully meet the challenges of leading the global organization.

INTRODUCTION

In the past decade bookstore shelves (or perhaps more appropriately e-book and audiobook download lists) have been filling up with books about globalization, working globally, leading globally—and the list goes on. Succeeding in a global context is no longer a business strategy to gain a competitive edge; it is a business imperative in order to stay in the game.

The pieces in this fieldbook will help you explore the core issues and ideas about what it takes to lead yourself, others, and your organization in a global context. Different topics and diverse perspectives are presented, but underlying it all is the core capacity of learning how to adapt to and navigate in a global context.

This book is comprised of revised and updated versions of articles originally published in CCL's magazine, *Leadership in Action*, between 2000 and 2010. It is the fourth installment in CCL's *The* Leadership in Action *Series*; the first three are titled *On Strategic Leadership, On Leading in Times of Change,* and *On Selecting, Developing, and Managing Talent.*

The book offers a mosaic of wisdom and is organized in a way that allows you to focus on your particular area of interest or need, and although you do not need to read the pieces in sequential order, each piece offers unique value and is worth reading. Following are brief summaries of some of the perspectives found in this volume:

- In "Global Managing: Mastering the Spin of a Complex World," Christopher Ernst describes four pivotal capabilities: international business knowledge, cultural adaptability, perspective taking, and innovation. These key capabilities are the global manager's axis—the knowledge, motivation, and skills needed to be effective and adaptable amid the complexity of the global marketplace.

- In "Challenge Match: The Stakes Grow Higher for Global Leaders," Shannon Cranford and Sarah Glover share six themes that emerged from interviews with forty senior global leaders from thirteen countries. The leaders were asked to describe their best and worst experiences in their global leadership roles and to give advice and opinions about how to lead in a global setting. This piece distills the information gleaned from the interviews into practical advice.

- In "For Global Managers, a World of Difference," by Maxine A. Dalton, Jennifer J. Deal, Christopher Ernst, and Jean Brittain Leslie, the characteristics that contribute to high performance by global managers are presented. The authors also offer suggestions for ways organizations can recognize and foster those characteristics.

- In "Leading Globally Requires a Fundamental Shift," Ancella Livers underscores that although many executives recognize that moving into a global position requires them to manage under multiple sets of laws, currencies, and time zones, many don't understand that leading in a global setting requires a fundamental shift in their thinking and behavior. Executives have to understand that their ability to lead effectively is often determined by their followers' willingness to follow, and they also have to recognize that they are embedded in multiple layers of complexity.

- Michael H. Hoppe, in "Adult Development Theory May Boost Global Leadership," raises an adult development perspective on global leadership as a means to help us realize that the majority of leaders function at a developmental level that rarely does justice to the complexities, diversity, and changes around them. He describes three stages of adult development—moving from dependent to independent to inter-independent—with the latter two levels including and integrating but also surpassing the previous level(s), and he applies them to leadership.

- In "Global Leaders Face Challenges in Asia," Sam Lam and Mohit Misra indicate that although much has been written about leadership issues in Asia, the focus has generally been on the context in which businesses operate and the critical role of understanding that context, building trust, and leveraging relationships. They acknowledge that these are legitimate points, but suggest that they are a gross oversimplification. Leaders in Asia need a sound grasp of the three C's: context, content, and creativity.

- In "Getting to the Source: Four Perspectives on Leadership," David V. Day and Patricia M. G. O'Connor focus on how leadership is accomplished in a global context. They describe how different perspectives correspond to four leadership models: leadership by a strong individual, a hierarchy, a pipeline, and collective practices.

- Hal Richman and A. William Wiggenhorn, in "Hatching a Plan: Developing Leadership Talent in Emerging Markets," posit that there is a lot of talent waiting to be developed—and a lot of risk if this doesn't happen. They also offer actions that organizations operating in emerging markets can take to strengthen their homegrown leadership pools.

- In "Across the Boards: How Chairmen's Roles Differ Around the World," Andrew P. Kakabadse notes that board of directors chairmen have a wide range of responsibilities important for organizational success. But he also discusses a survey that discovered that practices of chairmanship and board dynamics differ around the world, and the implications of that finding for organizations in the United States, the United Kingdom, and Australia.

- In "Bridging Boundaries: Meeting the Challenge of Workplace Diversity," Christopher Ernst and Jeffrey Yip propose that in a globally diverse and increasingly interconnected world, social identity boundaries rub together, pull apart, and collide in the workplace, and that when these identity divides open up, people look to leaders to bridge the gaps. The authors describe four tactics for bridging the gaps: spending, reframing, nesting, and weaving.

- In "Cultural Intelligence and the Global Economy," Joo-Seng Tan notes that the abilities to adapt constantly to different people from diverse cultures and to manage the interconnectedness of today's world are critical. The global workplace requires individuals to be sensitive to different cultures, to interact appropriately with people from different cultures, and to analyze new cultures as they are encountered. To do all this, individuals, whether they are at home or abroad, need cultural intelligence, which is a person's ability to successfully adapt to new cultural settings—that is, unfamiliar settings attributable to cultural context.

- Maxine A. Dalton, in "Cultural Adaptability: It's About More Than Using the Right Fork," acknowledges that adapting to the cultures of the countries in which managers conduct business is a crucial capability, but also notes that it is an often misunderstood and oversimplified capability. As global managers work at adapting to other cultures, they need to be mindful of issues of appropriateness and ethics. This piece provides a useful framework for doing so.

- In "One Prescription for Working Across Cultures," Craig Chappelow offers a simple and familiar dictum to apply when visiting and working in other countries: "First, do no harm." It boils down to using basic manners, employing self-awareness, and monitoring one's behavior. In this piece, he shares a multitude of specific and often humorous stories based on his experiences working in different cultures.

- In "Getting the Message: How to Feel Your Way with Other Cultures," Don W. Prince and Michael H. Hoppe describe how the discomfort you feel when cultural boundaries collide can be used to your benefit by alerting you to cultural differences. The authors also note that when you work and conduct business with people of other cultures, your cultural biases can emerge with more force when triggered by this discomfort. They recommend staying with uncomfortable experiences and learning from them, and they offer specific examples and advice about how to do this.

- The GROVEWELL-CFGU Partnership, in "Gaining a Critical Edge in Mastering Globalization," suggests that the lessons learned in pursuing diversity and inclusion within a U.S. setting are, to some extent, applicable worldwide. But it recommends that intercultural consulting needs to be part of the approach as well. Together, intercultural consulting along with diversity and inclusion offer business leaders a critical edge in mastering globalization.

- In "If It's *Lagom*, This Must Be Sweden," Kristina Williams and Kay Devine describe Swedish leadership styles as an amalgamation of egalitarianism and consensus. They contrast the Swedish value of *lagom*, or "just enough," with the North American value of "more is better" and use that to illustrate Swedish leadership styles in specific ways.

- Elizabeth Weldon, in "Seeking a Model for Leadership Development in China," shares the results of a survey about Chinese leadership and how it differs from leadership in North America. She offers three conclusions. First, building strong bonds based on collaboration, teamwork, dignity, and trust is a key element of both Chinese and North American leadership. Second, like North American leaders, leaders in China believe that one of their main roles is to improve the company; North American leaders, however, place more value on experimentation and taking risks. Finally, although Chinese leaders believe it is important to help others succeed, they also believe that this is of secondary importance.

That concludes my whirlwind tour of all this volume has to offer. Now it's your turn to decide where to go first and dive in.

Kelly M. Hannum
Director, Global Research Insights
Center for Creative Leadership

Part I

BECOMING A GLOBAL LEADER

Global Managing: Mastering the Spin of a Complex World

Christopher Ernst

As the global economy has come of age, many managers have been thrust into leadership roles in which their skills don't match the requirements of the job. But are the capabilities needed to succeed in a global context really so different from those that are critical for domestic managers? And if there are differences, what can be done to develop these new skills?

As a high-level manager at a U.S.-based manufacturing company, Matthew leads a number of teams. He has just been asked by his boss to turn over responsibility for one of those teams to someone else and take on a different task—managing a new plant in Frankfurt, Germany. The factory was recently acquired in a merger and there's a lot riding on its success, so Matthew views his selection to manage it as a vote of confidence and another feather in his cap.

He starts to imagine what his life would be like as an expatriate. But reality stops him short—after all, his boss didn't ask him to move to Frankfurt. He didn't even ask him to spend a lot of time there. Instead, the boss wants Matthew to continue to manage his domestic teams as he always has and at the same time use the tools of technology—e-mail, videoconferencing, faxes, and the like—to connect with and direct his new team in Germany. The boss says Matthew needs to meet face-to-face with his people in Germany only occasionally.

Matthew believes that although his new task will mean some additional work and an increase in the scope of his job, he'll be able to manage his new team in much the same way he has managed his domestic teams. But he's in for a shock. He is about to take on a job that is not only bigger but far more complex.

Global managers are faced with a range of new challenges. They must become integrators of performance results, business acumen, social patterns, and perpetual technological advances, not only in their home bases but around the world. They need to acquire a new set of skills to effectively meet these complex challenges.

For many organizations, succeeding in the global economy has risen to the top of their agendas, and global managers are increasingly being asked to lead the way. And yet many managers find themselves in Matthew's situation—thrust into a global

leadership role in which their skills don't match the requirements of the job.

What are those requirements? Are the skills required for success in managing a global operation completely different from those needed to effectively manage a domestic operation, or do they overlap? And what can organizations and leaders do to develop the skills needed to excel in a global context? CCL research work with a group of managers (see "Global Versus Local: Comparing the Requisites" on next page) produced some insights that go a long way toward answering these and other questions.

GRAVE NEW WORLD?

For global managers to get a firm grasp of the challenges they face, they must first develop a realistic picture of the new, expanded, and diverse environment in which they operate and how it differs from the relatively homogeneous setting of the domestic manager.

In the best-seller *One World, Ready or Not: The Manic Logic of Global Capitalism* (Simon & Schuster, 1998), political writer William Greider provides a lucid and vivid description of the crucible in which novice global managers find themselves. It is a world in which managers are required to process, integrate, and make decisions based on huge amounts of disparate information; to negotiate with governments that have very different notions of how business should be done; to interact with a complex web of organizational relationships in multiple and diverse countries; to recruit and develop the best talent from anywhere in the world; and to develop strategic alliances—even with competitors that operate within different models of capitalist systems. Stir all of these ingredients together and one gets a sense of the ambiguity and stress inherent in globally complex work.

Through its research, CCL has identified several dimensions across which the global manager must work simultaneously—even if, like Matthew, the manager spends the majority of his or her career behind a desk at the home office.

Global Versus Local: Comparing the Requisites

In an effort to learn whether managers with global responsibilities and those with purely domestic responsibilities need
different types of knowledge and capabilities to be effective, CCL
conducted a study of 214 managers from thirty-nine countries
working in thirty countries around the world. The managers'
companies represented four industries and had corporate
headquarters in Sweden, Switzerland, and the United States.
Half the managers had local responsibility (they directed operations within the borders of one country), and half had global
responsibility (they directed operations in multiple countries and
across various cultures).

The managers completed a number of questionnaires
comprising nearly 1,000 items, and each manager's boss completed a questionnaire about the manager's job effectiveness.
CCL researchers then conducted a series of correlational analyses
and found that there is one set of capabilities that all managers
need to be seen as effective by their bosses whether their work
is global or local in scope. These are the essential capabilities—
core business knowledge; the ability to cope with pressure; and
the ability to manage people, action, and information. More important to the objectives of the research, CCL also identified four
pivotal capabilities that are uniquely related to the effectiveness
of global managers—*international business knowledge, cultural
adaptability, perspective taking,* and *innovation.*

Geographic distance. Global managers must be able to deal
with the inconveniences of time differences and the practical
and psychological difficulties of not always being able to see the
people with whom they work.

National infrastructures. Global managers must negotiate
multiple and sometimes antithetical variations in political and

economic systems, regulatory and legal frameworks, and civic and labor practices.

Cultural expectations. Global managers must familiarize themselves and comply with a wide range of sometimes startling expectations in regard to behavior—their own and that of their colleagues, employees, customers, suppliers, and distributors—and the ways in which work should be done.

The complexity faced by global managers grows exponentially with the number of countries, cultures, and time zones in which they work. During teleconferences, for instance, each participant could well be in a different time zone. A global manager at a meeting in Tokyo must be aware not only of Japanese exchange rates, corporate culture, laws, investment policy, and labor unions but also of the infrastructures of each other nation in which his or her company does business. When a global manager gets off a plane or sends an e-mail message, a different set of cultural expectations awaits at the arrival gate or the recipient's computer monitor. Constantly confronted with such Byzantine situations, it's no wonder that global managers can often be reduced to conducting reality checks—asking themselves, "Where am I?" or, "Who is that sitting across the table from me?" rather than the most critical question: "What do I need to do to be effective in this context?"

What these managers need to sort out the massive and manifold input of a complicated world is more than just a firm command of the *essential capabilities* that are required of all managers to be effective, whether their work is global or local in scope. They must also learn to nurture and attain four *pivotal capabilities* that are uniquely related to the effectiveness of global managers.

TURN, TURN, TURN

Think of the axis on which a globe rotates. Just as the globe spins on its axis, the global manager adapts to fluid, complex situations by using the pivotal capabilities—*international business knowledge, cultural adaptability, perspective taking,* and *innovation.* The pivotal capabilities are the global manager's axis—the knowledge, motivation, and skills needed to be effective and adaptable amid the complexity of the global marketplace. Global managers who develop the pivotal capabilities are less likely to become immobilized by that complexity.

International Business Knowledge

To be effective, global managers must have a solid understanding of how business is conducted in each country and culture where they have responsibilities. On the big-picture level, international business knowledge means having a thorough grasp of your organization's core business and how to leverage that business within and across each country where your organization has markets, vendors, resources, and manufacturing operations. On the grassroots level, it means knowing the laws, histories, and customs of each of those countries.

Gaining international business knowledge involves taking classes, reading books, and talking with experts. Being sophisticated in the realm of international business not only gives global managers the savoir faire to behave appropriately and stay out of trouble, it also guides them in developing a broad, long-range strategy and keeps them aware of how decisions at one location affect possibilities and outcomes at others.

But intellectual knowledge goes only so far. No matter how prestigious a manager's education and how thorough the data the manager receives from the organization's information technology, human resources, and legal departments, such knowledge is of limited value if the manager can't use it to adjust personal behavior to various business contexts and to help co-workers do the same. To capitalize on international business knowledge, global managers must also pay attention to the other pivotal capabilities.

Cultural Adaptability

Global managers must act on their knowledge of cultural differences and use that knowledge to help them interact effectively with people from different cultures. A large part of cultural adaptability is being able to deal with the stress and the perceptions of eccentricity and strangeness that can arise from global complexity.

For instance, a U.S. global manager who faces an important deadline on a project in Mexico may notice during a teleconference that the team members in Mexico seem unconcerned as they deliver an overdue status report. Cultural adaptability would allow the manager not only to know that Mexican business tends to be conducted under a different time orientation than is common in the United States—in Mexico, people take precedence over schedules—but to act on that knowledge in an appropriate way. Similarly, cultural adaptability would allow a female global manager in Europe who is negotiating with a Saudi Arabian to use her knowledge of the role of hierarchy, class status, and gender in Saudi culture and to adjust her words and actions accordingly.

In an article published thirty years ago in the journal *International Studies of Management and Organization,* Indrei Ratiu of the global business school INSEAD, which has campuses in France and Singapore, was one of the first to examine the role of cultural adaptability in determining the success of global managers, or *internationalists.*

One characteristic of successful internationalists, wrote Ratiu, is that they begin with general knowledge, or prototypes, of cultures when they first start dealing with those cultures. As they get to know people from those cultures as *individuals,* however, successful internationalists are able to let go of or adjust elements of their prototypes and gain a less stereotypical knowledge of the cultures and their people. Unsuccessful internationalists either don't start off with prototypes (and as a result interpret everything based on their own mental frameworks) or are unable to discard their prototypes despite evidence culled from their interrelationships with people from other cultures that ought to dispel preconceptions.

Managers who are culturally adaptable, then, sign on to the notion that logic and truth are relative. In her book *International Dimensions of Organizational Behavior* (Thomson South-Western, fifth edition, 2008) Nancy J. Adler, a professor of organizational behavior at McGill University in Montreal, writes that "in approaching cross-cultural situations, effective business people . . . assume differences until similarity is proven. They recognize that all behavior makes sense through the eyes of the person behaving and that logic and rationale are culturally relative."

This view can create tension for global managers, however, especially if they tend to approach the business world as a nuts-and-bolts environment of budget sheets and Pareto charts. To ease this tension, global managers need to develop the next pivotal capability.

Perspective Taking

Everyone has a personal perspective—images of and beliefs about what things are and should be. But not everyone is adept at taking the perspectives of others—seeing and understanding their views of what things are and should be.

There are several idioms that give a sense of what is meant by perspective taking: *Walk a mile in my shoes. I know where you're coming from. I see what you mean.* All of these show that there is a large element of empathy in perspective taking. In the case of global managers it is *cultural* empathy—knowing, understanding, and acting in accordance with the deeply held values and beliefs of people from other cultures.

Imagine that you and a friend are hiking up a steep, wooded slope. As you near the summit, you both stop to catch your breath and look back at the view. Your friend says she can see a town over the treetops. But she is ten yards ahead of you, and you can see only the trees. Because you and your friend are standing in different places, you literally have different points of view. To see what your friend sees, you must move to where she is standing, and vice versa.

Of course, walking up or down a hill to see the view from a different perspective is easy. Understanding how to act, communicate, and lead while taking into account the perspectives of colleagues, direct reports, and customers from other cultures is not so easy.

Whether the context is global or is confined to a single culture, the processes and behaviors involved in perspective taking are largely the same: listening to and absorbing information skillfully, recognizing that other people's views of a situation may be different from yours, understanding that other people's assumptions about what things are and should be may be different from yours, and accepting the limitations of your own point of view.

Yet implementing these processes and practicing these behaviors can be especially difficult for managers operating in a global context, because they do not have the luxury of working from a single, commonly understood cultural framework. The frame of reference held by each individual with whom global managers deal, and which they must strive to understand, changes from culture to culture.

An example of how fundamentally different cultural perspectives can be was offered by Erica Goode in her August 8, 2000, *New York Times* article "How Culture Molds Habits of Thought," which reported on a study of U.S. and Japanese managers who were asked to look at the same picture and describe it. The U.S. managers tended to talk about the people in the picture, whereas the Japanese managers were more interested in the setting of the picture. The study underscored how two people looking at the same thing will often focus on different aspects of it because of their cultural perspectives.

Developing the ability to distinguish the moods, temperaments, and intentions of people from other cultures requires a concerted effort, especially in the virtual environment in which global managers typically work. Global managers who interpret and label the behaviors of others based on their own cognitive and interpersonal frameworks will be more likely to make mistakes about others' motivations, and their own actions and reactions will be liable to leave other people shaking their heads. However, global managers who learn to take the perspective of others and to reorganize their own sense-making frameworks will grow to see multiple perspectives as not incompatible but as all having potential for contributing to solid managerial decisions and actions. Such managers will make sense to, rather than confound, the people from other cultures with whom they work.

Global managers who add the final pivotal capability—innovation—to the first three will have the tools not only to understand and adapt to the complexity of the global business environment but also to capitalize on that very complexity to achieve success for themselves, their teams, and their organizations.

Innovation

For global managers, the role of innovator is integral to the other pivotal capabilities. Only through skill in innovation can global managers take their knowledge of international business, understanding of cultural differences, and ability to experience the perspectives of others and leverage them to create something new—a new policy, procedure, product, service, or practice—that is greater than the sum of its parts.

In this respect, innovation is the most essential of the pivotal capabilities. It takes managers beyond merely managing the complexity of global operations to turning that complexity to their advantage.

Building skill as an innovator is a step-by-step process of gathering information, learning to listen and pay attention, letting go of the need to always be *right,* and seeking out useful combinations.

Examples of skill in innovation can be found in the realm of music. In the 1960s the Beatles' George Harrison developed an interest in Indian culture, religion, and music. It wasn't just a passing fancy; he took lessons from sitar virtuoso Ravi Shankar and immersed himself in the culture and traditions of India. The knowledge Harrison gained, his cultural adaptability, and his willingness and ability to take a different perspective led him to write and record songs that transcended both the rock and classical Indian genres—they were an entirely new type of music that was neither Eastern nor Western. Similarly, Paul Simon became captivated by the stirring harmonies of the a cappella group Ladysmith Black Mambazo during a visit to South Africa in the mid-1980s and incorporated their traditional sounds into his album *Graceland,* which fused a number of styles into a completely new one. The innovations of both Harrison and Simon are credited with creating and popularizing *world music,* which is not a *type* of music in the traditional sense, like blues or jazz, but is rather a hybrid of any number of combinations of musical styles from around the globe.

An example of innovative skill in a business context is found in the story of a British manager assigned to set up a manufacturing plant in an impoverished area of Africa. He had hoped to recruit a reliable and loyal workforce, but many employees weren't showing up for work. In an attempt to solve the problem he began offering free lunches to workers. But absenteeism continued to be rampant and was severely cutting into the bottom line. Unwilling to reconcile himself to a constantly revolving workforce, the manager brought into play his pivotal capability of perspective taking by talking with the local tribal leaders to try to get a handle on the problem. He learned that the workers didn't feel justified in coming to the factory and being fed while their families were left hungry at home. The manager innovated by serving lunch each day to workers *and* their families. The cost was more than offset by the fact that absenteeism all but disappeared.

SEEKING THE NEW

As a set, the pivotal capabilities provide the knowledge, motivation, and skills that global managers need to master the spin of a complex world. Developing these capabilities requires continually seeking out new and varied experiences that challenge your current perspectives and offer new ones. There are many possibilities for such experiences, but here are some that have proven effective for global managers:

- Study new languages, not primarily to gain fluency but rather to become familiar with their syntaxes and structures. This can be a powerful way to understand and appreciate how people from other cultures think.

- Make a habit of arriving a day or two before a business meeting in a country you have never visited before. Hitting the streets, interacting with merchants, and tasting the local cuisine are simple yet effective ways to orient yourself to other cultures and their people.

- Read the literature and listen to the music that are popular in a country you're getting ready to visit. This gives you a deeper and richer understanding of the culture than you can get from skimming a guidebook.

- Host foreign visitors in your home, and get to know people in your own country who are of different ethnicities or religions.

- Read as much of the international business press as time allows.

With globalization increasingly the norm and as advances in information technology become even more rapid, the world of international business will become only more complex. Developing the pivotal capabilities and establishing a synergy among them will enable global managers to stretch to meet this challenge, and increase their chances of achieving success for themselves and their organizations.

Challenge Match: The Stakes Grow Higher for Global Leaders

Shannon Cranford and Sarah Glover

Leading globally is extremely complex. The differences between the requirements of leadership at a local level and leadership at the global level are exponential. To learn about the specific challenges faced by global leaders, CCL conducted interviews with senior global leaders. Analysis of the responses revealed six common themes.

Paying special attention to the relatively new and unique problems and challenges of global leadership is vitally important for two reasons: power and complexity. Global and multinational organizations have enormous power; their influence and impact shape the world—socially and environmentally as well as economically. An article in the September 2004 issue of *Harvard Business Review*, "How Global Brands Compete," detailed the results of a study that found that consumers around the world see global brands as so influential that they are responsible and obligated in ways that local brands are not. The stakes are much higher in international business, so people expect more from global leaders. As a result, considerations that once seemed insignificant and that leaders never had to worry about before can make or break a company's reputation and a global leader's career—and affect the bottom line.

Consider the following true story:

A newly promoted international sales director, Carl, was criticized by his boss for not meeting sales goals. Carl then conducted an emergency conference call with members of his sales network, who were located in several different countries. The sales network included Carl's sales managers as well as members of some of the company's distribution partners. In an effort to be results oriented and to motivate his sales network to achieve better financial results, Carl was very aggressive in his communication, repeatedly taking a bullying line of attack. This tone had been successful for him in the past in getting his U.S. colleagues' attention and impressing on them the urgency of the situation. As Carl delivered this diatribe, he didn't realize that some members of his sales network in Argentina were becoming extremely offended; they felt their value and contributions were being degraded and disrespected. In their culture, professionals simply did not speak this way to one another. As a result, one of the distribution partners ended its relationship with Carl's company and went over to the competition. Other distributors in on the conference call voiced similar concerns about partnering with an organization whose leaders used such an approach.

Eventually the CEO of Carl's company got involved and sent a Latin American executive to patch things up in person with the distributors and reestablish the working relationships; ultimately the conflict was resolved, and the remaining distributors kept their relationships with the company.

Carl soon realized he had made incorrect and damaging assumptions about what motivated members of his sales network. His actions had been instinctive, automatic, and habitual. After the fact he saw that the stress of the situation had caused him to forget all his book learning about working across cultures. Under the gun he had relied on a strategy that had previously worked in his own culture and context.

Leading globally is extremely complex. The differences between the requirements of leadership at a local level and leadership at the global level are exponential. In *Success for the New Global Manager: How to Work Across Distances, Countries, and Cultures* (Jossey-Bass, 2002), Maxine Dalton, Christopher Ernst, Jennifer

Deal, and Jean Leslie refer to research that found that all managers whose responsibilities are limited to a single country must be able to manage action, information, and people; must have business knowledge; and must be able to cope with pressure. The authors go on to explain how each of these managerial requirements mushrooms in complexity at the global scale. The basic leadership processes of setting direction, generating alignment, and maintaining commitment are all harder to do across cultures, distance, and time. In other words, it's *the same, but different.* There are more inputs to decision making and they often overlap and conflict with each other, and the outputs have more consequences and must please more stakeholders. There's more ambiguity and potential for crossed wires, which can slow productivity, diminish morale, and result in conflicts that waste time and social capital.

Planning for complexity and uncertainty includes understanding and paying attention to potential dangers and to who your stakeholders are. Because of the volatility of global business, leaders can't make decisions ahead of time, but they can research the choices and possibilities, familiarize themselves with the issues, and plan for different scenarios. If they do these things successfully, when the pressure is on they won't have to struggle with each question for the first time—they will be better informed and can focus on adding new data from the immediate context to their decision-making process.

SIX THEMES

What are the specific challenges faced by global leaders? To shed some light on this question, CCL conducted interviews with forty senior global leaders from thirteen countries in Asia, Europe, the Middle East, and North America. Although the study had a small sample, it is just one part of CCL's research aimed at understanding the issues and problems inherent in global leadership. The leaders were asked to describe their best and worst experiences in their global leadership roles and to give advice and opinions about how to lead in a global setting. Analysis of the responses revealed six common themes, which complement previous research in this area:

- Managing the relationship between corporate headquarters and local offices
- Understanding and managing external forces
- Handling cultural conflicts
- Adapting one's own behaviors
- Creating shared goals and implementing shared work
- Communicating across barriers

As the world of international business touches more and more lives and as technological changes continue to enable quick decisions (and equally quick repercussions), all managers in all organizations can benefit from building a greater awareness of the challenges inherent in global leadership roles. The lessons to be learned are about interdependence, paradox, and priorities.

Managing the relationship between corporate headquarters and local offices

This challenge involves balancing operating under dynamic local conditions with protecting the organization's overall welfare. Leaders at all levels tend to feel the tension between the demands of global consistency and local differentiation. A regional director in a multinational corporation, for example, must follow global mandates that come from the top but still take into account the local context and the concerns of local employees.

One of the interviewees in CCL's study described the instructions he received from his company's U.S. headquarters during a round of layoffs, telling him to let go of contract employees first. This would have made sense in the United States, where there is less organizational commitment to contract employees than to permanent staff. However, the instructions violated accepted practice in other countries where seniority counts more, regardless of employment status (contract or permanent).

How can global leaders manage the inconsistencies, conflicts, and continual adjustments arising from the combined global and local contexts so that their organizations continue to thrive? One way is to avoid taking a one-size-fits-all approach to setting global strategies that must be implemented regionally. Local offices should have the flexibility to integrate themselves according to the customs of the regions in which they are located. Setting norms or guidelines that allow both headquarters and local offices to give and receive input on decisions can help achieve this flexibility. A corporate code of conduct that applies to all locations can also be a useful unifying and clarifying tool. It is critical to learn both the local laws and the informal customs for doing business in all the countries where your organization operates, even when international law or your global corporate culture supersedes local ways of doing things. You will at least learn what local employees are used to and may expect. You can also use this knowledge to develop your negotiation skills and your skills as an innovator.

Ask and listen. Observe reactions to and comments about corporate decisions and communications. Find out how corporate messages are understood and misunderstood in each location. Ask how policies set by headquarters might be different if the headquarters were in a different country.

Although recognizing the need for appropriate degrees of adjustment to local business models and workforce expectations is important, it is equally important to recognize the external forces at play that can affect organizational performance.

Understanding and managing external forces

Effective global leaders must recognize the various governmental, legal, historical, and economic factors that can influence how the organization operates. Even though leaders usually have little if any control over these factors, they must be taken into consideration when setting global and regional strategy so that appropriate tactics can be applied and executed according to local conditions.

One of CCL's interviewees with global leadership responsibilities in several countries emphasized the importance of being able to navigate through common business challenges such as exchange rates and international and federal issues related to trade balances, national policies, and the current political landscape. Global leaders must learn to make decisions in ways that mitigate any negative effects these external forces might have on a company's ability to do business.

One U.S. interviewee working in South Korea shared the following perspective:

> *One of the first things I would warn about when doing business in Asia is that there are significant differences country to country as far as their development level. There are a lot of national rivalries, a history of invasions and domination. The different levels in individual skills and abilities country by country are related to the economic maturity of that particular country. For example, if you have a group of people from mainland China versus a group of people from Singapore or Hong Kong, there's going to be a very wide gap between skill sets.*

Managing effectively in the face of pressure from external forces is one area where book learning can help global leaders. They can find out which external factors affect the strategy and operations of their organization in each location. These factors include governmental, legal, political, and economic conditions. Awareness of current sociopolitical issues and historical contexts in the different regions is important. These are the types of issues that affect the way decisions are made and the ability to do business. At the same time, it is important to not rely solely on official, written information. Ask people in different locations about their experiences and strategies for success.

Leaders must also avoid the mistake of looking at the economic factors too broadly and thinking of the countries in Europe or Asia or North America as homogeneous.

Handling cultural conflicts

Effective global leaders learn how to detach somewhat from their personal beliefs without losing their core identities. Priorities and values differ across cultures but don't have to lead to conflict. Effective global leaders also learn how to leverage different perspectives and turn them into opportunities for better meeting organizational strategy.

A Turkish manager working in Belgium explained this approach:

> *There are different paces in different countries, different maturities of your customer base and of the local management, so when you lead in different countries you have to take care of those differences. There is a velocity that is different by country, which sometimes you need to harmonize; there are skills that are different. When I think of my colleagues working in Russia, by no means can they sell the most advanced products to that market. Meanwhile you are a stock-traded company and you need to communicate with your stakeholders and to communicate those differences and manage expectations as a global leader. To simplify the image, if you think of different countries as wheels, they run at different speeds, and you need to harmonize that and understand the differences.*

In managing cultural conflicts, there is also the question of how effective leaders can be when facing fundamentally different norms and behaviors in working with people from different regions of the world. A Spanish executive working in Japan explained the difficulties of managing through the discrimination against women that still exists in some countries while keeping her organization's best interests in mind:

I was involved in negotiating local contracts and restructuring the operation. In the Japanese culture there is no room whatsoever for a female executive to deal one-on-one with her counterparts. They absolutely ignored me. I let the regional director lead negotiations and I took a back-seat position. I would instruct him beforehand about the conditions I wanted and then sit and watch the negotiations. I was very uncomfortable and I was naturally furious, but I was there to achieve certain results. Training courses don't prepare you for that. They are always about learning to find common ground and turning differences into something positive. They don't teach you about the real conflict you will find as a global manager and what actions you need to take.

How can leaders wade through differing cultural behaviors effectively to achieve results that are best for their organizations? Here are some ideas:

- Espouse respect for cultural differences as a corporate value, so that this respect is explicitly sanctioned across the organization.

- Foster a climate of learning through initiatives—such as establishing communities of interest or sponsoring open discussion forums for sharing knowledge—that create cultural knowledge assets across the organization.

- Look for similarities first rather than differences.

- Link any cultural awareness or diversity initiatives to the strategic objectives of the organization. This enables staff at all levels in the company to better connect cultural diversity to organizational decision making and thereby their own work.

- Establish a relationship with mentors; lean on others who have the experience and knowledge to provide guidance and advice.

Developing the ability to skillfully manage cultur
can also help leaders develop the capacity to adapt their l
to the composition of the workforce.

Adapting one's own behaviors

Most global leaders can relate a story about a time when
they had to consciously change particular behaviors to adapt to
a different culture or region. All of CCL's interviewees had some
comment about the necessity of being open-minded, understanding the culture you are in, or having an international mind-set.
How does one notice one's own ingrained habits, recognize the
need to change them, and then actually make changes?

An American global automotive supplier, for instance,
changed the type of car he drove in deference to his biggest client.
A Dutch manager working in a regional office in the Middle East
said he adapted his overall management style. He had always been
a hands-on type of manager but now stands back more and lets his
local managers do the hands-on work. He said the challenge was
to find an appropriate level of steering that would be helpful while
not interfering on a day-to-day basis.

Here are some other ideas for adapting your own behaviors:

- Get feedback on your behavior, both as it currently is and
  on your attempts to change it. Ask specific questions.

- Practice changing your behavior. Learn a new skill, whether at work or as a hobby. Implement new habits you have
  wanted to develop, and practice being adaptable. When
  appropriate, try another person's way of doing something
  just for this purpose.

- Allow your plans to be changed at the last minute.

- Notice what helps or hinders you in adopting new
  behaviors.

- Observe others for reactions when you are interacting
  with them, and consciously adapt your words or deeds

to match the cues they give you (for example, boredom, impatience, or interest).

- Find and study a role model or mentor. Is there someone already displaying the kind of behavior you want to display? Observe that person keenly. Get to know that person, if possible, and ask how he or she goes about producing this behavior.

- Travel and put yourself in new situations.

- Consider putting yourself in the situation of being a minority if this is not an everyday experience for you.

- Reduce stress whenever possible. Stress and pressure can cause you to revert quickly to old habits, and they also limit your ability to observe and absorb new information.

Creating shared goals and implementing shared work

Sometimes shared goals and shared work involve deliberate strategies used to bring different groups together across cultures or locations, and sometimes they are simply a fact of life.

Several of CCL's interviewees related experiences in which shared goals or projects were successful either despite of or because of global diversity. Such goals and projects included events as simple as meetings and gatherings held to jointly celebrate something, such as the launch of a new brand. One interviewee, however, described how complex projects that involve people in different locations can result in differing agendas and perspectives. The result is often a gradual departure from the overall objective.

To establish a strong sense of shared goals and shared work, it is important to take a number of actions:

- Effectively communicate the big picture—what the larger goals are and the reasons for pursuing them. This helps employees better connect their work to the common goals and objectives of the organization.

- Keep the overall goal clear and simple enough that it can be repeated and restated by everyone involved.

- Tie each goal or task to larger goals that group members share.

- Consider developing and implementing a structured method of participative decision making. Deciding by majority vote is one method, but for some situations—particularly those that involve diverse groups of people from different locations—it is important to establish a method of gaining consensus. It is important to facilitate a group's ability to reach common ground and attain buy-in from all involved.

- Clarify the situations in which shared goals and shared work are appropriate. Elucidate who is in charge of making decisions and who will be rewarded or penalized for specific outcomes. Create joint accountability for tasks and goals—teams should be rewarded or reprimanded as groups.

- Take time to celebrate shared accomplishments. Demonstrate that the organization values shared work. Be careful to not underestimate the importance of team building. Recognize that any time someone joins or leaves a team, it becomes a new team. Diversity can be a great asset for teamwork—for innovation or problem solving, for instance—but it requires more time for team building.

Communicating across barriers

Sometimes it can feel as though there are more barriers than openings in the landscape of global leadership. The most common barriers that can trip up global leaders are not necessarily related to geography, with all its varying legal and political restrictions, but to language and culture, which can hinder effective communication. CCL's interviewees identified barriers of distance, geography, time zones, language, and culture. Effective global leaders recognize the barriers to effective communication and learn to either eliminate them or work around them, resulting in common understanding and clarity of communication.

A U.S. executive working in South Korea elaborated on the implications of working across time zones:

> *When everyone is operating in his or her local time zone, you have a twelve-hour or worse time difference. You have people operating with "morning mind" and others with "late evening mind," and my experience is that this can affect things profoundly as far as the energy of the participants.*

A Dutch executive working in the United Arab Emirates had a more positive view of working with colleagues in other time zones:

> *I thought that working across different time zones and by telephone and video would be a pain, but I have found that if I have a bit of telephone and computer discipline, I can download data and e-mail to my computer before I board a plane, then work on the plane, and when I arrive send messages. I thought it would be a nightmare; however, I am surprised that it works well. Taking advantage of the tools available to work as a virtual team is key. I set rules with my colleagues to respect one another's time. I use technology and try to see the human person on the other end.*

Communicating across barriers is one of the more obvious challenges of global leadership and the activity that can have the most impact when managed effectively. It is critical to communicate objectives and expectations in an explicit manner to ensure common understanding. Be clear on your targets, goals, and expectations. Leaders should make a conscious effort to pause and ask such questions as "Does everyone understand what I mean when I say . . . ?" A leader's ability to reach beyond communication barriers is a fundamental element of a global mind-set.

A Turkish manager working in Belgium explained this dynamic:

If I ask a Belgian to draw a tree and a German to draw a tree, they would draw a tree but each would look very different. And neither is what the customer needs. Having common objectives and understanding the same thing when you are managing people in different countries is one of the most important things.

Some organizations find that a clear, explicit global protocol for e-mail communication—for example, guidelines on who should be included in the address line in order to respect cultural norms regarding hierarchies—helps managers avoid frustrations.

Also, the burden of working across time zones should be shared. If one team always seems to be taking calls in the evening, try doing it the other way around half the time.

A WAY OF LIFE

CCL's research also found that leaders in different regions differed in their main challenges.

- European leaders reported challenges in the communicating-across-barriers category more than leaders from other regions did.

- U.S. leaders identified understanding and managing external forces as their most frequent challenge.

- Middle Eastern leaders said their most common challenges were communicating across barriers and managing the relationship between corporate headquarters and local offices.

- Asian leaders reported a comparatively even distribution of the common types of challenges.

CCL's study underscores the fact that managing complexity is simply a way of life for global leaders. The potential to be overwhelmed is as great as the potential for impact. Though many factors are outside global leaders' control, these individuals are still in positions of enormous influence. The bottom line is that it's all about knowing what to pay attention to—being prepared in the face of the unknown and quickly making sense out of confusion in order to gain global agility.

For Global Managers, a World of Difference

Maxine A. Dalton, Jennifer J. Deal, Christopher Ernst, and Jean Brittain Leslie

Which traits, skills, and capabilities are most likely to be associated with high performance ratings for managers with global responsibilities, and are they different from the traits, skills, and capabilities linked to high-performing managers with domestic responsibilities? CCL research has uncovered some answers that can be applied in organizations to increase their global leadership capacity.

As more and more companies cross the border from a national to an international focus, the need for managers who can operate effectively in a global environment increases. In the course of a day a global manager might have to work with a plant manager in Asia, a supplier in South America, government officials in Africa, and strategic alliance partners in Europe. This presents challenges in communication, collaboration, quickness of action, and mobility that are far different from those faced by managers whose responsibilities are limited to a single country.

In this piece we will look at some of the characteristics that contribute to high performance by global managers and some of the things that organizations can do to recognize and foster those characteristics. But first one must have some insight into the complicated and constantly changing world in which global managers operate. Here's a look at a hypothetical morning in the life of a global manager:

John Mitchell is sitting at his desk in New York in May 1999. The phone rings. It is the Beijing plant manager, who is British, announcing that the factory has been shut down because the workers are demonstrating after the accidental NATO bombing of the Chinese embassy in Belgrade, Serbia. John accepts this information without comment. He knows the plant manager only slightly and is not sure whether the man is prone to understatement or hysteria. John has always found it hard to read the British.

After telling the plant manager to hold tight and await further instructions, John hangs up and turns to his e-mail. There is a message from a plant manager in Mexico. Inflation remains rampant, and employees are complaining that they don't make enough to pay their spiraling rent. John is mildly annoyed, thinking that Mexican managers act more like workers' parents than like supervisors. He responds to the message abruptly, then wonders whether he should have hit the send button.

John leaves his office to go to a meeting and passes the company's finance director in the hallway. The director tells him that relocation costs for expatriates are out of control. John barely hears him; he still has Beijing on his mind.

John turns back to his office to ask his secretary to arrange a conference call of all plant managers worldwide. The call will take place across twelve time zones. John knows he'll have to be up at 3 a.m. to participate in the call.

John's secretary reminds him that he will fly to Mexico on Monday for a five-day stay and then head to England, where he'll spend a week. She asks John if the conference call should be scheduled to take place before he goes or during his trip. (This year, for the third year in a row, John has acquired more than 100,000 frequent-flier miles. He wonders whether he'll ever get to use them or if he even wants to.)

John heads back out of his office to go to the meeting, at which he's scheduled to explain why there have been cost overruns in manufacturing.

WHAT IS A GLOBAL MANAGER?

John Mitchell is a global manager. He is not an expatriate. He lives in New York and his office is in New York, but he manages across distances, cultures, and countries through the use of the telephone, e-mail, and faxes. He frequently has to travel. Every time John picks up a phone, gets off an airplane, or checks his e-mail, he is faced with a management issue. This is true of any manager, but John must assess and respond to each issue through the ever shifting lenses of distances, countries, and cultures.

When John manages across distances, he is dealing with the inconvenience of time differences and the significant practical and psychological difficulties of not being able to see the people he works with. When John manages across countries, he must deal with differing laws, political systems, and economies. When he manages across cultures, he must deal with differing expectations about how he should behave; how employees and colleagues should behave; how customers, suppliers, and distributors should behave; and how work should get done. Because John works with plant managers in many countries and each country has a different culture and is a different distance away from his New York office, his job is extremely complex.

GLOBAL MANAGERS' ROLES

In a multiyear study of four organizations with headquarters in the United States or Europe, CCL asked 214 managers located in thirty countries which roles and capabilities were most important in their jobs. Each organization is in a different industry sector: high-tech manufacturing, services, pharmaceuticals, or vehicle manufacturing. Half the managers have primarily domestic responsibilities and half have global responsibilities. Each manager was asked to rate the importance of seven role behaviors and eight capabilities to being effective in his or her job.

with domestic responsibilities rated the role of importance to being effective in their jobs than ith global responsibilities. Managers with global rated the roles of spokesperson and liaison higher in importance to their jobs than did managers with domestic responsibilities. Managers with global responsibilities also rated the capabilities of cultural adaptability, international business knowledge, and time management significantly higher in importance to their jobs than did managers with domestic responsibilities.

The research results indicate that when managers are in the same location as their subordinates—in which case the likelihood is high that the managers and subordinates are members of the same cultural group—the traditional role of leader is perceived as highly important. However, when managers are not in the same location as the people they manage—in which case the likelihood increases that the managers and subordinates are members of different cultural groups—the roles of liaison and spokesperson, along with the ability to be culturally adaptable, the capacity to manage time, and the specialized knowledge needed to conduct business internationally, assume greater importance.

These are the role behaviors and capabilities that managers themselves identify as most important to their jobs, but some additional information emerged when managers were viewed through the eyes of other people in their organizations.

THE HEART OF PERFORMANCE

Which traits, skills, and capabilities are most likely to be associated with high performance ratings for managers with global responsibilities, and are they different from the traits, skills, and capabilities linked to high-performing managers with domestic responsibilities?

A manager brings to his or her job certain personality traits, knowledge, experiences, and skills. We wanted to examine all these factors, so we set out to look at the whole person.

We wanted to find out whether any personality traits, any skill at playing particular managerial roles, and any specific sets of capabilities are more likely to be associated with good performance when a manager's work is global in scope than when the work is domestic in scope. (We judged performance according to how each manager's boss and direct reports rated the manager in five areas of performance.)

Personality Traits

Previous research has established two personality traits as being especially important to managerial effectiveness. CCL's research reached the same conclusions. Managers who are emotionally stable and conscientious—meaning high achieving and dependable—are more likely to receive high performance ratings from their bosses and direct reports than are managers who do not possess these traits. This is true whether the manager's work is global or domestic. As a sidelight, it is interesting to note that these two personality traits emerged as strongly related to managerial effectiveness even though the managers in the study represented more than thirty nationalities.

The research found no personality trait that is uniquely and directly related to effectiveness for managers with global responsibilities as opposed to those with domestic responsibilities. However, the study did uncover relationships between particular personality traits and specific skills that may have implications for developing effective global managers. We examine those relationships later in this article.

Skill in Playing Managerial Roles

We found that whether managers work in a global or a domestic context, their skill in playing the roles of decision maker, spokesperson, and negotiator has a bearing on performance ratings from bosses and direct reports. The abilities to take action, solve problems, take responsibility, weigh consequences, and resolve issues in the face of risk and uncertainty are key to performance whether the scope of the work is global or domestic. Global managers, however, must adapt *how* they negotiate, represent the company, and make decisions to each country and culture they deal with.

Also, skill in playing the role of innovator was found to be related to performance ratings only for managers whose jobs are globally complex. Innovators are managers who know when it is critical to see things in new ways, try new approaches, and seize new opportunities. Ronald A. Heifetz, in his book *Leadership Without Easy Answers* (Harvard University Press, 1998), speaks of innovation as a possible outcome when worldviews collide. The work of global managers is by definition caught between opposing worldviews. The ability to meet this challenge through innovation can help determine a global manager's effectiveness.

Specific Sets of Capabilities

We looked at three sets of capabilities—learning capacity, knowledge, and resilience—to see if any aspects of these capabilities have an impact on the performance of global managers but not on the performance of domestic managers. We found that being adept at perspective-taking—seeing the world through someone else's eyes—is a characteristic of higher-performing global managers but has little impact on the ratings of domestic managers. Similarly, the degree of specialized knowledge of international business is a factor in the performance of global managers but not of domestic managers.

The ability to cope with pressure is related to performance for all managers, whether global or domestic.

FLEXIBILITY IS KEY

To sum up, managers in international organizations, whether their responsibilities are global or domestic, need to be able to assume the roles of decision maker, spokesperson, leader, and negotiator.

Global managers, however, must have the flexibility to play these roles differently when dealing with different cultures and to cope with the associated stress and pressure. Additionally, managers who manifest the traits of emotional stability and conscientiousness are more likely to be rated as high performers.

When a manager's work shifts to a global scope, he or she needs to be able to play a new role, that of innovator. To be successful the global manager must be able to take the perspective of others and must possess and put to use a specialized knowledge of international business.

For managers making a transition from domestic to global responsibilities, it is perhaps their skill in the role of innovator and their capacity for perspective-taking that largely determine how successful they will be at taking the skills and capacities that were critical in their domestic jobs and adapting and leveraging them in their global jobs.

BENEFITING FROM THE RESEARCH

We believe that the findings of CCL's research can be applied in organizations by managers in global roles, by managers aspiring to global roles, and by human resource development professionals to design systems that prepare others for global roles. If you apply our findings in your organization, you should evaluate how the research work is playing out in your industry, with the people in your organization, and in different contexts.

How does one acquire the skills and capabilities to be an effective global manager? Traits and experience are central to development of skills and capabilities. Managers learn the skills that allow them to be effective from a host of experiences, including assignments, relationships, and education. It is likely that each person comes into the world able to learn some sets of skills with less work and effort than other sets of skills.

We explored whether any personality traits might be associated with particular skills and whether any cosmopolitan experiences—such as having lived or been educated in a number of countries or having learned more than one language—might be tied to skills that were found to be uniquely critical to the effectiveness of global managers.

We uncovered some connections between certain personality traits and particular skills, knowledge, and capabilities. Managers who were skilled at playing the role of innovator were more likely to have the traits of openness to change and of extroversion. (Extroversion is what allows them to "sell" the innovative approach.) Managers who were adept at perspective-taking were more likely to have the traits of emotional stability and agreeableness—which includes trust in and consideration for others, candor, and sympathy. Managers with a high degree of international business knowledge were more likely to have the traits of emotional stability and conscientiousness.

Does this mean that people who do not have the traits of agreeableness, openness to change, extroversion, conscientiousness, and emotional stability can never acquire the skills needed to be effective global managers? No; it merely means that managers seeking to acquire new skills or play new roles can benefit from knowing who they are. This self-knowledge prepares them to understand how difficult it will be to acquire a skill or play a new role, and it helps them map a learning strategy.

We also found connections between cosmopolitan experiences and the skills and capabilities unique to global managers. Managers with international business knowledge were more likely to have the skill of cultural adaptability and to be able to take the perspective of others. They were more likely to speak multiple languages, to be widely traveled, and to have lived in a number of countries. We also found that global managers who had extensive experience interacting with diversity in their previous domestic work experience had higher levels of international business knowledge.

The links between these cosmopolitan experiences and the skills and capabilities critical to being an effective global manager have implications for executive development. Organizations could gain a competitive advantage by identifying their most likely future global executives early in their careers; providing them with language training, expatriate opportunities, and the chance to serve on or manage virtual and cross-cultural project teams; and sending them on international business trips.

DISAGREEMENT ON A GLOBAL SCALE

One interesting finding from CCL's research is that global managers' performance ratings from their bosses often conflicted with the performance ratings from their direct reports, whereas the level of agreement between bosses' and direct reports' ratings of domestic managers was similar to that found in most multi-rater exercises.

The inconsistency in the ratings of the global managers was likely rooted in the fact that most of the direct reports were not in the same country or from the same culture as the managers. It underscores the dilemma of global managers: their direct reports are scattered around the globe, hold a wide range of cultural expectations about how the managers should behave, and work in different business contexts. It also underscores the qualities that are core to the effectiveness of global managers: cultural adaptability, the ability to see the world through others' eyes, innovativeness in the midst of opposing worldviews, and a thorough understanding of doing business internationally.

CCL's research found a paradoxical dark side for managers who are perceived by their bosses as being cosmopolitan. Being multilingual, being widely traveled, and having lived in a variety of cultures are critical factors in developing the skills needed to be an effective global manager, but these same factors are associated with negative ratings from bosses in one area of interpersonal relationships. Managers who fit this highly cosmopolitan profile are rated low by their bosses on how well-liked and trusted they are by their peers and other colleagues in their organizations.

We were initially puzzled by these findings but found a possible explanation in a 1983 article in the journal *International Studies of Management and Organization* by Indrei Ratiu of the global business school INSEAD. In "Thinking Internationally: A Comparison of How International Executives Learn," the author notes that internationalists are seen as being extremely effective but also as "chameleonlike," in a negative sense. So the very experiences that help global managers learn to be flexible and innovative may also contribute to their being disliked and mistrusted by other people in their organizations. Understanding and adapting to this phenomenon is just one more challenge for the global manager.

Leading Globally Requires a Fundamental Shift

Ancella Livers

Global leaders who have moved from a domestic or regional leadership role must manage an ever-shifting swirl of cultural behaviors, regional needs, and corporate expectations while also dealing with the challenges all leaders must face. They also need the technical know-how to manage across time zones, currencies, languages, and laws. All this requires a basic change in their thinking and behavior.

It was after Nirve's parents came to the job interview that René realized the shift to global leadership would present more changes than he had anticipated. In René's country such meetings were for the job applicant only. For Nirve, however, bringing one's parents and sometimes even grandparents to the potential workplace was normal, even expected.

Such gaps between different people's expectations can have a significant and often unanticipated impact in the global leadership arena. Leaders who consider themselves ready to take on the business challenges inherent in operating around the world often do not consider and are unable to predict the kinds of leadership challenges they will face.

Although many executives recognize that moving into a global position requires them to manage under multiple sets of laws, currencies, and time zones, many don't understand that to *lead* in a global setting requires a fundamental shift in their thinking and behavior.

As leaders increasingly take on global roles, it is becoming clear that the skill sets required for effective global leadership include not only well-researched and well-understood competencies but also abilities that take leaders across an exciting, sometimes frightening, new frontier. It is almost a cliché to say, for instance, that global leaders must be adaptable and open to new ideas. However, knowing that one must be adaptable and actually being adaptable are very different things. In truth, leaders often struggle to grasp the intricacies of leading groups of people from around the world.

Further, executives have to understand that their ability to lead effectively is often determined by their followers' willingness to follow. Consequently, when leaders' styles are alien to their followers' experience, the leaders will either have to modify those styles, educate their followers about those styles and hope the followers are willing to change their own leadership expectations, or face the prospect and even likelihood of an ineffective leadership tenure.

To be sure, leaders who work in their home countries and have solely domestic responsibilities can also find leading an organization to be complicated. There are various views to consider and numerous challenges and sometimes time zones that must be managed. However, because these leaders are working in their native countries, the cultural attitudes, expectations, and assumptions—including assumptions about leadership—are usually clear.

When one is leading regionally, across national lines but within a defined geographical area, leadership becomes more complex. In such circumstances, leaders are called on to negotiate different business practices, cultural tenets, and languages even as they juggle the leadership expectations of their followers. Yet, as difficult as regional leadership can be, the countries within a region often share enough basic, overarching cultural understandings to make even highly divergent behaviors vaguely familiar. Beyond this, countries within a region often have long histories of dealing with one another, and their citizens are acclimated to each other's idiosyncrasies.

In moving into global leadership, however, leaders must deal with a significantly higher number and degree of boundary-

spanning complications and thus must negotiate thro
complexity, ambiguity, and diversity than is found in
domestic or regional context. New global leaders ofte
a passing cultural, historical, and business familiarity with those
with whom they interact and lead and so have little in the way of
true understanding about what they must do to successfully navigate their new circumstances.

This intense environment of multiple layers of complexity
and perspective results in *multiplexity,* a term that highlights the
profound shift in the circumstances under which global leaders
must operate. As global leaders, executives must manage an ever-
shifting swirl of cultural behaviors, regional needs, and corporate
expectations while also dealing with the challenges all leaders must
face. Further, these leaders must also exhibit the technical know-
how to manage across time zones, currencies, languages, and laws.

To lead effectively, executives must set a clear direction, create alignment within their organizations, and gain and maintain
commitment among those who are led. These tasks become more
difficult as the leader moves from a relatively homogeneous workplace to a more heterogeneous one. Consequently, to successfully
enact these leadership responsibilities within their organizations,
global leaders have to gather information and understanding by
gaining multiple perspectives, building common ground, leveraging differences, and acting in a context of multiplexity.

Many executives believe that leading globally simply means
doing more of what they were doing domestically or regionally. At
a very basic level, this is true. The tasks of setting direction, creating alignment, and gaining and maintaining commitment are critical for all leaders. But if leaders approach global leadership merely
as they did domestic or regional leadership, they set themselves on
a road that will likely limit their efficiency and effectiveness.

Leading in the context of multiplexity does not change the
goal of leadership—creating a thriving unit or organization—but
it fundamentally changes how leadership is manifested and understood in order to meet that goal. To believe otherwise may be

ɔmforting, but it is not supported by either research or practice. To embrace multiplexity and all that it entails is to take the first step to becoming not only a global leader but a global citizen.

Adult Development Theory May Boost Global Leadership

Michael H. Hoppe

Individuals in global leadership roles need help acquiring the necessary experiences and requisite skills to succeed. Research in the field of adult development points to the potential for deriving a framework for global leadership development from this field. An adult development perspective on global leadership may make us realize that the majority of leaders function at a developmental level that rarely does justice to the complexities, diversity, and changes around them.

Anyone in a global leadership role has been given a tall order. The nature of the global leadership environment—increasingly volatile, uncertain, complex, ambiguous, culturally diverse, intricately intertwined, and advancing technologically at breakneck speed—causes many individuals in global leadership roles to ask: "Am I in over my head? Do I have the mental, emotional, and behavioral wherewithal to ever get a firm grip on this work? And if so, how can I best get to that point?"

What is often behind these questions is the acute sense that, to paraphrase Albert Einstein, we cannot hope to tackle the problems and opportunities of this new work environment with the same competencies and mind-sets used to create it—that we need to develop and apply ways of thinking and acting that at a minimum are at the same level of complexity and interconnectedness as the challenges and opportunities before us.

An example from the realm of technology illustrates this idea: an effective computer software engineer possesses one set of skills and mental capacities; an expert computer network manager has acquired a broader mind-set, additional competencies, and more inclusive frames of reference in order to be effective when integrating multiple networks across distances, countries, and cultures.

We need to find ways to help individuals in global leadership roles have the necessary experiences and acquire the requisite skills to succeed. This process will naturally include challenging job assignments, such as working on international projects and working outside of one's own culture. Moreover, global leaders need to be provided with opportunities to reach levels of individual growth that do justice to the levels of job complexity and human diversity that are hallmarks of their work. That task in itself requires a framework for leadership development that is conceptually and empirically sound and that can guide the development of individuals who are likely to succeed as global leaders.

The literature reporting on recent research in the field of adult development points to the potential for deriving such a framework for global leadership development from this field. There is clearly promise in applying an adult development perspective to the development of global leaders.

The main finding of this adult development research is the existence of predictable stages of development or distinctly identifiable levels of consciousness or internal *action logics,* the various principles that we use to construct our understandings of self and that noticeably shape how we interpret our surroundings and react when our power or safety is challenged. These principles, by extension, guide the ways in which we understand others and our relationships to them. Moreover, they are conceptually and empirically different from common notions of intelligence in that they are concerned with the various ways in which we make sense of the world around us. In general, then, an adult development perspective postulates that we have the potential to develop increasingly complex levels of understanding of ourselves and the world in which we live, to broaden our behavioral repertoire, and to widen our inclusiveness of those who are different from us.

THREE STAGES

An overview of the literature on adult development by Cynthia McCauley, a senior fellow at CCL, and colleagues identifies three stages of adult development, moving from *dependent* to *independent* to *inter-independent,* with the latter two levels including and integrating but also surpassing the previous level(s).

In the context of a global work environment, individuals who use the dependent sense-making lens are deeply embedded in their own, their society's, and their organization's needs, traditions, values, and practices and tend to apply them as the measuring sticks for everything and everyone else. These individuals struggle to recognize that their thoughts and actions are learned, tend to think in terms of either-or, and perceive difference as a threat to themselves. They see change as a necessary evil.

Global leaders who think and act from the independent stance see themselves as the product of their past experiences, education, and culture. As they seek to grow toward their unique selves, they are curious about other individuals and cultures. They feel comfortable enlarging their own and their organization's boundaries to create mutually satisfying and productive relationships. They experience change as natural.

At the inter-independent level of functioning, global leaders look for the greater good, whether it's defined as that of their company, their customers, or humanity as a whole. They tend to think and act beyond predefined categories of culture, gender, religion, or social class and attempt to create systemic conditions that enable them and others to constantly transform. They embrace change and difference.

One of the implicit propositions in applying this theory to leadership development is that individuals will become more effective in their global leadership roles as they grow beyond the dependent stage. The descriptors of the dependent stage suggest that it is difficult to succeed in a global work environment unless one has reached (or at least is in transition toward) the independent level.

In an article in the April 2005 issue of *Harvard Business Review*, "Seven Transformations of Leadership," David Rooke and William R. Torbert describe how they found in their studies of thousands of managers and professionals that those at the dependent level were noticeably less successful in implementing organization-wide strategies than those at the independent stage were.

McCauley and her colleagues concluded that a growing body of evidence supports the view that leaders operating at the independent level are more likely than those operating at the dependent level to enact leadership in ways deemed effective in most modern organizations.

According to Rooke and Torbert, leaders at the inter-independent level show the most consistent capacity to innovate and successfully transform their organizations. However, at present it's hard to tell whether leaders at the inter-independent stage of development are the ones best suited and prepared to deal most effectively with the complexities, exceedingly fast changes, and cultural diversity of the workforce, clients, and constituencies in today's global work environment. So far the literature has identified only a small percentage of respondents who have reached the inter-independent level.

There is another reason for not automatically elevating the inter-independent stage to a prerequisite for effective global leadership: effective leadership requires what could be called effective *followership*. What happens when leaders' and followers' meaning-making structures are so far apart that they can't connect?

HOW TO HELP

How can we apply an adult development framework to help the majority of global leaders get their arms (and minds) around their work? A first step is to recognize the promise of this perspective. As Rooke and Torbert state, most developmental psychologists agree that what differentiates leaders is not so much their philosophies of leadership, their personalities, or their styles of management as it is their internal action logics.

A second step is to develop better and more efficient and user-friendly assessment instruments to gauge the meaning-making structures of individuals who are currently in or are on track for global leadership roles. This will, in turn, help us better understand which developmental activities best move individuals to the next developmental level. We know how some of these movements—for instance, from the dependent to the independent level—can be set in motion: a promotion and the resulting greater responsibilities, a realization that the old ways of doing things just don't work anymore, an expatriate assignment, or participation in formal development programs. However, we need to become more deliberate and structured in leader development work.

A third step is, seemingly paradoxically, to go beyond the preoccupation with *individual* leader development. We need to develop in equal measure the capacity and the developmental level of groups, organizations, communities, and societies as a whole to deal with the increased volatility, uncertainty, complexity, ambiguity, and diversity in the environment and the speed of technological change. It would be beyond the abilities and stamina of most of us as individuals to succeed in an environment that uses action logics that are not reasonably well aligned with our own or with the problems or opportunities at hand. Another part of this third step is to broaden our thinking regarding the source of leadership. What if leadership could be seen to be as much a property of the collective as of the individual?

An adult development perspective on global leadership may make us realize that the majority of leaders function at a developmental level that rarely does justice to the complexities, diversity, and changes around them. Could it be, then, that we must let go of the image of the individual leader who has it all and can do it all? Might we be better off if we increasingly think of leadership as something that we do together and share and for which we acquire the mental, emotional, and behavioral competencies that enable us to lead together to bring about a better team, organization, or community for the benefit of society worldwide?

Global Leaders Face Challenges in Asia

Sam Lam and Mohit Misra

As Asian markets have emerged as prime areas for business growth, much attention has been focused on the challenges faced by leaders of global companies in Asia. These leaders need a sound grasp of the three C's: context, content, and creativity. Thus far the first C has been emphasized while the other two have been almost completely excluded.

Perhaps the best examples of the challenges faced by leaders of global companies are found in Asia. Asia is attracting a lot of attention in the business world, and for good reason. China's continued economic growth (although that growth slowed in 2012 and the first quarter of 2013), India's ongoing economic reforms, and the steady development of the Association of Southeast Asian Nations have made Asian markets the ones where the prospects for business growth are most real and apparent.

Much has been written about leadership issues in Asia, and the focus has generally been on the context in which businesses operate and the critical role of understanding that context, building trust, and leveraging relationships. These are legitimate points, but they are a gross oversimplification.

Leaders in Asia need a sound grasp of the three C's: context, content, and creativity. Thus far the first C has been emphasized, to the almost complete exclusion of the other two. A few decades ago, when markets were unsophisticated and relatively closed, the availability of products from foreign multinational companies was a novelty, and foreign executives with even a perfunctory contextual understanding of the market and the business and cultural moorings of the country in which they operated could make the grade. That is no longer the case. As markets have opened and consumers have grown more sophisticated, they have come to demand more in terms of the value delivered to them. Understanding context is no longer enough; now, leaders and their organizations need to excel at content and creativity to be successful.

#2 By *content* we mean a sound understanding of the foreign country's infrastructure and value chain, from product conception to delivery to the client. For example, most multinational companies with a presence in India envision the profit potential presented by a middle-class consumer population of 250 million. But many of these companies fail to take into account that only one-fifth of that number can be reached through existing distribution channels. Companies that have succeeded in India have built deep marketing and support networks in rural areas. The best-laid plans of many consumer goods companies have gone awry because of a lack of understanding of the infrastructure and support mechanisms that allow products to be moved from the manufacturer to customers.

To make an impact in markets around the world, leaders of global companies also need to come up with *creative,* innovative ways to reach out to customers. Companies with operations in foreign countries often face stiff local competition. Fast-food chains, for example, find themselves going up against local cuisines that are entrenched through age-old tradition. The best approach is not to resist or go against the grain of tradition but to find creative ways to package products so they suit local tastes. McDonald's, for example, has had considerable success with a vegetarian burger in India.

In essence, leaders of organizations that have global operations need to concentrate not just on external factors such as branding and securing customers but also on internal factors such as building organizational capacities and capabilities. The big challenge in Asia is for leaders to fill the needs of various targeted populations through mass customization without escalating costs unduly. Only through a thorough understanding of not only context but also content and creativity can they make that happen.

Getting to the Source: Four Perspectives on Leadership

David V. Day and Patricia M. G. O'Connor

In the midst of all the innovative business strategies being deployed to respond to globalization, one fundamental aspect often remains unexamined: *how leadership is accomplished.* What are the most prevalent forms of organizational leadership and their relative strengths and weaknesses, and how can a leader reflect on the type of leadership found in his or her organization and whether that approach is the most appropriate for attaining the organization's strategic goals?

Globalization has brought about both previously unimaginable opportunities and significant and complex challenges for many organizations. The opportunities include increased innovation, better identification of emerging markets, development of new talent and material resources, and most important, a higher global standard of living. Along with these benefits have come some significant challenges associated with aligning across diverse cultures, governments, regulatory environments, and monetary policies. Global organizations are trying to leverage the diversity of ideas, opportunities, and contexts offered by the global arena while at the same time avoiding excessive fragmentation resulting from these differences. All of this is happening in an overall business climate that is increasingly competitive and complex.

In the midst of all the innovative business strategies being deployed to respond to globalization, however, one fundamental aspect often remains unexamined: *how leadership is accomplished.*

What are the most prevalent forms of organizational leadership and their relative strengths and weaknesses, and how can a leader reflect on the type of leadership found in his or her organization and whether that approach is the most appropriate for attaining the organization's strategic goals?

To help answer these questions, we considered the case of a Southeast Asia–based manufacturing company whose strong growth has led its executive team to contemplate a merger. Interviews with four members of the team formed to establish how to proceed on the possible merger discovered four very different perspectives on the source of leadership in the organization. These perspectives correspond to four leadership models: leadership by a strong individual, a hierarchy, a pipeline, and collective practices.

These four models range across a continuum running from power concentration to complexity. At the least complex and most power-concentrated end of the continuum is the leadership model dominated by strong senior leaders, often with leadership concentrated in a single individual at the top—typically the company's founder, president, or CEO. At the most complex and

least power-concentrated end of the continuum is the collective, or shared, leadership approach.

The four leadership models can be compared to each other across a number of criteria: the underlying business imperative that motivates the company; the relative strengths and weaknesses of each approach; the temporal orientation of each model in terms of past, present, or future; and the ways of facilitating and furthering the development of each approach.

Excerpts from the interviews with the executive team members highlight the distinguishing features of each leadership approach.

THE STRONG INDIVIDUAL (SOURCE ONE)

The interviewee speaking here is the manufacturing company's executive vice president of finance.

> *It's pretty clear to me that this is the CEO's call. He started this company from the humble surroundings of his apartment. He knows the company better than anyone. Although I'm sure he would be open to input—and of course I'll advise him on the financials—it has to be his decision, not only whether we should consider a merger but also who we should ultimately align with. The board holds him accountable for the company's performance. He is who the employees rely on to make the company number one. They are committed to his vision and they work together to make it happen because he has always chosen directions that resulted in great things for the company. Besides, since mergers and acquisitions are so complex, we need the clarity of one voice. And that voice is the CEO's.*

In this model the top-level leader, such as the company CEO or president, is considered to be *the* leader. Others in the organization look to this individual to solve all the organization's most complex problems and provide all the requisite leadership. In many cases this individual is the founder of the firm. Historically this has been the most prevalent leadership model, especially in founder-run organizations. It is the most common way that employees recognize leadership in such firms.

THE HIERARCHY (SOURCE TWO)
The interviewee is the executive vice president of product development.

> *I have learned the hard way that you've got to get every one of our fourteen senior directors to sign off on decisions like this. We expect them to deliver on goals set for the company by the executive team. This merger is going to affect every one of them in terms of changes to their span of control, the depth of their resources, and the stretch of their production targets. They will be held accountable for implementing whatever decision is made and, more important, communicating to their direct reports why we are doing this. If just one of them does not sign off on this merger, the whole place could grind to a halt. So we have to build in lots of time to send the particulars of this transaction up and down the chain of command. Once the directors see their fingerprints on the direction of this thing, they will commit to making it happen and will get their people aligned. Without that, this merger will go nowhere.*

This hierarchical model of leadership extends the strong individual approach in that there is no single, omnipotent leader, but position still matters. Leadership power and influence are concentrated into formal positions throughout the organization. Another term for this type of organization is *bureaucracy*. Positional roles are highly defined and relatively inflexible. Those who hold formal positions are solely responsible for the leadership of the organization. Those who are not in such formal positions are not considered to be leaders. Chain of command is a central feature of this model.

THE PIPELINE (SOURCE THREE)

The interviewee is the CEO.

> *When I begin to think about the implications this merger has for our future, it really gives me pause. This represents the introduction of a whole new phase for the company. It's going to change our fundamental business model. As such, everything might have to change—our assumptions about future products, the business practices we have relied on, and how we work together to make this new organization successful. Given the time it takes for mergers and acquisitions to truly impact all levels of the organization, success or failure is going to rest largely on the shoulders of future directors, not just the current ones. I can't imagine not tapping the perspectives of our next generation of leaders—that is, the thirty high potentials we have formally recognized through our succession planning process. We need to understand their ideas and concerns about this merger. We need to ask them what they think this merger is going to require of us as a company and of them as individuals. And of course we need their energy and commitment toward whatever merger candidate we ultimately choose. This is a turning point for the company. We have to leverage all our leadership talent to do this right.*

In this pipeline model, succession planning dominates the leadership strategy of the organization. Resources are provided to develop individual leaders who are prepared to handle senior-level positions when role vacancies occur. Another term used for this type of leadership model is *bench strength*—having many individual leaders who have been developed to handle leadership challenges and are now waiting on the sidelines. There may be questions, however, as to how much focus has been given to developing the leadership capacity of these individuals while they were developing their abilities to address role-specific technical challenges.

COLLECTIVE PRACTICES (SOURCE FOUR)

The interviewee is the executive vice president of sales and marketing.

> *I have read about the high failure rates of mergers, and it seems that we need to go into this with our eyes wide open. What did the organizations that successfully merged do that the others did not? I'm sure it is important to assess the leaders in the two organizations—do we have the skill and the experience bank to sustain the new enterprise? We also have to look at the technical strengths of each company. For example, what functions might the other organization excel at that we don't, and vice versa? What's less clear to me are some of the intangibles. For instance, what are some of the perhaps taken-for-granted practices and assumptions in our company and in the target company, and are these compatible? We currently have pretty straightforward decision-making processes in this organization. Everyone knows who needs to be involved and at what stage. What if the other organization is more ad hoc in terms of how it makes decisions? Also, we are more or less a family around here. What if the other organization doesn't value the relationships we've developed and doesn't know how to fit in? Finally, much of our reputation and success is a result of extensive and repeated dialogue about who we are today and who we need to be in the future. Even though the CEO has strongly influenced this process, he really encourages us to challenge our assumptions about the identity of the company. He believes we can change in response to industry demands and yet still preserve a core part of who we are. Who will we be after the merger?*

In the collective practices model, leadership capacity is distributed throughout the organization, with the focus on relationships among individuals and groups and on shared practices that produce leadership. Leaders *act with* others around them in creating leadership, rather than merely *acting on* others. Collective leadership practices recognize that it's critical for organizations to develop capacity in three areas: encouraging interaction among various people, functions, and constituencies as sources of identity and knowledge; driving the ability to learn from differences and to engage paradoxes; and treating inquiry into the identity of the organization as a path to bringing about useful change.

HYBRID MODEL

The interviews with members of the top-management team at the company we studied reveal that they have markedly different views on how the leadership of the organization should proceed on the potential merger. The executive vice president of finance sees the decision as completely in the realm of the CEO (the strong individual), the executive vice president of product development sees a need for buy-in from leaders up and down the chain of command (the hierarchy), the CEO holds to a leadership model that is inclusive in terms of recognizing the talent that can be found inside the company (the pipeline), and the executive vice president of sales and marketing has an even more inclusive perspective that takes into consideration all the people who make up the company (collective practices).

These disparities indicate that regardless of the objective structure of the company, the practical reality is that the company is being run under a hybrid model in which these four key stakeholders hold different implicit leadership theories.

Organizations have imperatives at varying times and in varying degrees for accountability, stability, flexibility, and adaptability. For these reasons it may be less common (especially in large organizations) to have a "pure" leadership model than to have a combination of practices—a hybrid model of leadership. These forms are progressive and inclusive. So an organization that recognizes collective practices as the source of leadership in all likelihood also engages in pipeline development, respects the role of hierarchy in introducing a measure of checks and balances, and experiences the influence of strong individuals. This hybrid model is driven by both business imperatives and the various activities that influential members of the organization recognize as leadership. With this in mind, increased awareness of and explicit discussion of the leadership models operating in organizations could well help managers build greater leadership capacity.

Despite the noted differences in leadership theories among the example company's executive team, it is less important for these executives to understand how these theories were developed than to learn how to go about reconciling them. Now that their differences have surfaced, they have the perfect opportunity to begin a discussion on what the company wants in terms of its leadership—a discussion that might also help them identify the best potential merger partners. That is, given the apparent diversity of leadership views and implicit theories among members of the top-management team, what is desired for the future of the company? What is the leadership brand or identity that the company wishes to create to enable its future success? Merging organizations that have very different leadership cultures might quickly find themselves at odds on the fundamental leadership tasks of setting direction, building commitment, and creating alignment.

There may well be important tangible benefits to understanding the various leadership models people in an organization hold and then working to align those models more closely. Creating alignment is one of the central tasks of leadership, and aligning the ways people think can be a precursor to more cooperative action. A fundamental maxim in the field of organizational behavior is that thinking is for doing. Thus, thinking about leadership in ways that are more consistent and aligned across an organization may provide a foundation for leading more effectively across all functions and levels of the organization.

Hatching a Plan: Developing Leadership Talent in Emerging Markets

Hal Richman and A. William Wiggenhorn

Emerging markets, which have a strong economic growth trajectory and market opportunity, are of great interest to large global organizations. But there is a lot of leadership talent waiting to be developed in these markets, and a lot of risk if this development doesn't occur. Here's a look at some actions that organizations operating in emerging markets can take to strengthen their leadership pools.

Ashoka, the third monarch of the Indian Mauryan dynasty, who ruled in the third century B.C., has come to be regarded as one of the most exemplary and compassionate rulers in history. Ashoka had numerous inscriptions carved on stones and pillars throughout his empire, which included the current nations of India, Nepal, Pakistan, and Afghanistan. These edicts proclaimed Ashoka's reforms and policies and promulgated his advice to his subjects, such as the following, cited from *The Edicts of King Ashoka*, by Venerable Shravasti Dhammika (Buddhist Publication Society, 1993):

> *Everywhere has Beloved-of-the-Gods, King Piyadasi [Ashoka], made provision for two types of medical treatment: medical treatment for humans and medical treatment for animals. Wherever medical herbs suitable for humans or animals are not available, I have had them imported and grown. Wherever medical roots or fruits are not available, I have had them imported and grown. Along roads I have had wells dug and trees planted for the benefit of humans and animals.*

Ashoka's legacy offers insight into a powerful, compassionate, and insightful ruler's attempt to establish an empire on the foundation of what we might call "doing the right thing" by making the moral and spiritual welfare of his subjects his primary concern.

Cross-cultural training is part of many leadership development programs, but few programs get into the depth of Ashoka's.

Have Ashoka's principles ever been examined in depth by a prestigious Western business school or expert or formed the core of an executive development program promoting leadership competencies? What could leadership experts learn from Ashoka and how he lived and worked?

In this piece we will provide some background on emerging markets, raise some issues regarding leadership development in these markets, and pose some provocative questions.

LOOKING FOR GROWTH

Emerging markets are often defined by a series of indicators, such as stability of the political environment, degree of corruption, economic growth, physical infrastructure, social infrastructure, and maturity of civil society, that when taken together denote an economic growth trajectory and market opportunity.

Emerging markets are of great interest to large global organizations and other organizations with an international presence that have reached saturated growth in their traditional markets. These enterprises are looking for access to new markets, breakthroughs and innovation, access to local resources, market intelligence, speed to market, and sustainability of their market investment. Many of these organizations are also looking to emerging markets for growth of their global talent pools.

The statistics on the growth of emerging markets are interesting, with 12 percent of emerging markets representing 73 percent of the developing world's gross national products; 60 percent of growth in the developing world's population through 2020 will be in China, Brazil, India, and Mexico. Significantly, new market relationships are forming between Brazil and China and between India and China.

BIG CHALLENGES

Talent supply is a core competitive advantage of modern enterprises in growth markets. U.S. government studies show that among the companies in growth markets, 61 percent do not have the right people to be trained, 47 percent suffer shortages of leadership talent, and 40 percent do not know how to train their staff members to be world-class managers. In short, there is a lot of talent waiting to be developed—and a lot of risk if this doesn't happen.

A report by the National Center on Education and the Economy highlights a number of challenging issues for leadership in emerging markets. This study, based on more than two hundred interviews, points out that because engineers and scientists in China are accorded higher status than managers, there is a short supply of capable managers. This shortage generates a seller's market for qualified candidates, with constant job offers at higher wages, resulting in "foreign-capital firms paying native Chinese managers with the right skills and experience as much as they paid ex-pats to do the same work."

Another big challenge for enterprises in emerging markets is that they need to compress fifteen years of development and experience into five years, *unless* all the leadership talent is imported. They also need to develop trust and accountability at warp speed; keep the talent supply chain full in both good and bad economic cycles; and not be afraid to partner with major customers, suppliers, joint venture partners, and government agencies in sourcing and developing talent.

In India, comments Manohar Arcot, a leadership development consultant who previously was general manager of corporate human resource development for technology giant Wipro, "one of the ways the sector is tackling the shortfall in professional managers and other skilled staff is to partner with educational institutions, to help design and provide training and education programs. This way the 'hit rate' when hiring gets better. If we start early with them, we can help them get the training right. At Wipro, we also widened the net in terms of hinterland and strengthened internal training for technical and soft skills for managers. Many companies have started working with the educational institutions to set up huge university-type campuses. There is a concerted and ongoing effort to get the right people with the right skills."

Enterprises in emerging markets cannot assume they can mimic companies in developed markets, simply selling the same products and services and using the same distribution model. All the research and practice focused on the *bottom of the pyramid* (a phrase that refers to the fact that the billions of poor people in the world have great entrepreneurial and buying power; see *The Fortune at the Bottom of the Pyramid,* by C. K. Prahalad [Wharton School Publishing, 2005]) shows that the economics of emerging markets may require radically new views on how products and services are developed, sold, priced, and distributed. Such views require managerial leadership in many areas, including technology, research and development, business models, and management processes. This new managerial leadership needs to be willing to experiment, collaborate, empower locals, and create new sources of competitive advantage and wealth.

Yes, the challenges are great; however, the cost of *not* developing leaders in emerging markets is high. Consider the cost of ignorance, of lost market share because talent is not ready and available, of negative turnover because individuals with high potential are not being developed, and of perception in the marketplace that the organization does not develop talent.

SENSE OF TRUST

To develop their talent, companies operating in emerging markets can use a variety of standard learning, training, and development activities, including

- Stretching job assignments and increasing levels of responsibility early in the careers of key talent

- Engaging in meaningful action-learning projects (such as case studies and simulations) that are transferable to the job at hand

- Blending delivery of education, using technology, simulation, and peer-group study teams

- Providing trained mentors and coaches to correct specific gaps in competencies

- Making available developmental activities such as job rotation (including cross-organizational council and committee assignments), position shadowing, cohort M.B.A. training for select high-potential talent, and out-of-country travel for key talent

- Ensuring language proficiency via English language training for non-English-speaking employees and foreign language training for English-speaking high potentials

- Making it clear to employees that career prospects may not necessarily be limited to the home country

Learning, training, and development need to be multilateral for all groups of an enterprise around the world that will be working with emerging markets and not simply for leaders in the emerging markets. And all these actions need to create a greater sense of trust, so that local management is deemed trustworthy and trusts corporate management.

Arcot describes how development also contributed to employee retention at Wipro. "Factors such as clear visibility of employees' careers, challenge on the job, strong up-skilling processes, and the perception that an employer is a good place to work—they all contribute to attracting and keeping good people."

Eilif Trondsen, research director at Strategic Business Insights in Menlo Park, California, is a thought leader in learning and innovation. He says: "I think there is a huge opportunity to leverage the growing number of aging baby boomers who are now nearing retirement but many of whom might be very interested in serving as teachers, coaches, and mentors for emerging leaders in developing countries. Perhaps someone will organize a new type of 'peace corps' that focuses on training leaders in emerging countries by using some of the talent embodied in many of these aging baby boomers, many of whom would find such roles exciting and challenging. Also, there is plenty of technology that could be put to good use in supporting and enabling such remote leadership teaching, coaching, and mentoring to minimize the need for a lot of travel."

FIXING DYNAMICS

Global EduTech Management Group (GEM), a Chinese corporation, has established private co-op universities in China. GEM brings in instructors and curricula from prestigious universities such as Hong Kong Space University, Warwick University, the Rochester Institute of Technology, and the M.B.A. program at the University of Notre Dame to deliver degree programs recognized by the Chinese government. GEM's intent is to make its campuses a magnet for emerging leaders from around the world, not just China.

GEM's Experienced Commercial Leadership Program accelerates the development of commercial-savvy talent through a structured program combining coursework, job assignments, and interactive seminars. In China it is a two-year program consisting of four six-month, cross-segment assignments within the commercial function of a GEM business. Two of these rotations are focused on marketing and two on sales. Program participants strengthen their commercial, business, and leadership skills by completing an intensive curriculum consisting of eight weeks of classroom training, online training, and in-residence global symposiums. All program members complete one international rotation.

In the late 1990s, Motorola was faced with a problem in its labor-supply dynamics in China. Its China Accelerated Management Program (CAMP) was developed as a response to this problem. CAMP—based on a combination of action learning, coaching and mentoring, training, and job rotation—was an innovative and effective effort by Motorola to quickly train a sufficient number of high-potential, local Chinese employees to become middle managers in the short term and effective senior managers in the long term.

CAMP's knowledge-and-skills model offered a combination of functional and technical knowledge and administrative, cognitive, leadership, and communication and interpersonal skills, and also fostered personal adaptability and motivation.

Trainees' improvement, as observed by managers, included an increased ability to think in strategic and customer-focused terms; a better understanding of Motorola's culture and ways of doing business; and greater maturity in working with people, use of teamwork, and presentation skills.

Other companies that have successfully developed talent for emerging markets include Johnson & Johnson Medical, China; Procter & Gamble, China; Koch Corporation, Turkey; Emerson Electric, China; Unilever, India; Kuwait-Americana, Egypt; and the Hewlett-Packard Emerging Market Solution team.

ISSUES TO MULL

Some issues to anticipate when developing leadership in emerging markets include the need to hire on the basis of language capability rather than managerial and functional competency; the challenge of keeping people in their jobs long enough to learn from their actions; the importance of setting career-track expectations; the desirability of repayment agreements for advanced degree programs; the need to address mismatches between mentors and mentees and coaches and coachees; the importance of providing accurate and continuous feedback on total performance; and the need to be aware that ambitious local talent will be easily lured to opportunities offered by fast-growing homegrown rivals.

Interviews that we conducted with learning executives working in emerging markets produced some additional issues to anticipate:

- "Firms have various ways of attracting talent from emerging markets, including global recruitment firms, referrals from existing staff, and recent graduates from prestigious business schools," says Kong Chin, director of Ingersoll-Rand University Asia Pacific. "However, some firms, especially those from mainstream industries, have a very difficult time attracting talent in emerging markets and need to turn to specialized boutique recruitment firms." Kong adds that if the corporate culture is strong, it will overtake the languages, values, and business style of the national culture so that everyone "speaks the same language," but if the opposite is true, the national culture will predominate.

- KL Cheah, former director of Motorola University in the Asia Pacific region, believes it is also important to remove glass ceilings of all types. With respect to national and corporate business cultures, KL observes that the most resilient managers are those who can act like "chameleons," shifting their styles between the two cultures as needed.

- Stephen Krempl, president and cofounder of TriZenter LCC and formerly with Motorola and Yum Brands, observes that informal learning, such as that received through spending "face time" with counterparts at events, is important for fitting into the corporate culture. Krempl also believes that organizations need to start thinking of recruits as being part of the global talent pool (as opposed to an individual nation's talent pool) and to make corresponding adjustments in their learning, training, and development efforts.

PIONEERING CHANGE

Samantha Tan, originally from Singapore, has an M.Ed. degree from Harvard. She now is a partner with the Meristem Group, a Cambridge, Massachusetts, firm that provides leadership education to those serving the public interest. Also a member of an innovative worldwide network of emerging leaders called Pioneers of Change, Tan says that enterprises need to put more focus on emerging leaders.

Pioneers of Change is a global learning network of young people in their twenties and thirties who have committed to be themselves, do what matters, start now, engage with others, and never stop asking questions. The pioneers include social entrepreneurs, corporate and nongovernmental organization professionals, civil servants, artists, teachers, and free agents with a variety of cultural and social backgrounds. Founded in 1999, the organization has more than two thousand participants in more than seventy countries.

Some pioneers have been working at Kufunda Learning Village, an innovative learning, training, and experimentation center in Ruwa, Zimbabwe, dedicated to creating sustainable communities. Marianne Knuth, founder of the village, holds a master's degree in international business and economics from the Business School of Copenhagen. Despite her skills and training she will probably never be picked up on the talent radar of any multinational corporation; however, her resilience, daring, innovation, and insight would make her an incredible asset to a range of enterprises working in emerging markets, particularly those working at the bottom of the pyramid.

The Western business culture and cultural code—with their focus on action and use of language to manipulate the world—are becoming the norm. This has the potential to subvert thousands of years of learning and culture that could bring fresh insights to leadership and management. KL Cheah sees little research in this area of management and wonders how this ancient knowledge can be applied to modern management. The danger of not paying attention to this area is a cultural dumbing down in leadership and management training and practice, where the behemoth of Western thinking suffocates alternative, and potentially critical, ways of thinking. This would be bad for emerging economies and ultimately for the world.

In China one trend suggests that the leadership challenge is not being met: despite efforts to foster talent internally, multinationals are finding that their strategy of building local talent is foundering and that the talent they *have* managed to develop is being lost to the emerging Chinese corporations—where rising stars perceive the prospects of earlier and wider-ranging responsibilities as highly attractive and much better than those afforded by the multinationals. (Paradoxically, there is a move to attenuate the race to localize by bringing in more Chinese-speaking non-Chinese on local contracts—as opposed to traditional expatriate, package-based arrangements.) A secondary by-product of this trend, which could well become more pronounced over the coming decades, is the notion that Western-style management may eventually be supplanted (in China and in overseas Chinese operations) by a Chinese model of leadership that synthesizes a modified neo-Confucianism with a cherry-picked set of Western techniques that work in a Chinese context. As the dean of a leading business school in China says, "pick the best [of the West], discard the rest, and meld it with a north-Asian leadership view.

A leadership institute based in Pudong, Shanghai, the China Executive Leadersihip Academy, has been setting the pace by inviting cutting-edge leadership thinkers to China to imbue the business and political leadership of the country with fresh ideas that will be tried out in China, modified, and implemented. The prospect of new concepts of leadership emerging from China is very real and will affect the Western world in ways we can only now begin to envision. More Chinese leaders are beginning to challenge core Western assumptions about the way business should be conducted, and many point to what they see as the dehumanizing elements of management in the West—advanced, as they see it, by the dictates of business school experts and the preponderance of traditional Western thinking in M.B.A. programs.

A further prospect is that this new Chinese-led approach to leadership will resonate far beyond China to Japan, South Korea, and Taiwan, where concepts of social networks and interrelationships—traditionally disparaged, ignored, or misunderstood by the West—will eventually predominate. Western interest in learning about the view in China on business and leadership is gaining traction and is underscored by the popularity of programs that explain or interpret the Chinese approach. The GEM Close Up on New China program, for example, a two-week immersion for students in Western M.B.A. programs to learn about China and Chinese business culture, has proved to be a great success. Also to be expected is the emergence of a reflective, altruistic form of leadership from India, where it is no surprise to see eminent schools such as Harvard set up research facilities (Harvard's is in Mumbai) to tap into alternative ways of thinking that do not derive from the Western tradition.

An article in the 2005 Number 4 issue of *McKinsey Quarterly*, titled "China's Looming Talent Shortage," underscores the issues and challenges in leadership development in emerging markets. An excerpt from the article states:

> *Indeed, far from presaging a thriving offshore services sector, our research points to a looming shortage of homegrown talent, with serious implications for the multinationals now in China and for the growing number of Chinese companies with global ambitions.*
>
> *To avoid this talent crunch and to sustain its economic ascent, China must produce more graduates fit for employment in world-class companies, whether they are local or foreign ones. Raising the quality of its graduates will allow the country's economy to evolve from its present domination by manufacturing and toward a future in which services play the leading role—as they eventually must when any economy develops and matures. The conditions for a flourishing offshore sector will then surely follow.*

Across the Boards: How Chairmen's Roles Differ Around the World

Andrew P. Kakabadse

Board of directors chairmen have a wide range of responsibilities important for organizational success. But research has found that practices of chairmanship and board dynamics differ around the world. What are the implications for organizations in the United States, the United Kingdom, and Australia?

How important are the roles of chairmen of the board to the success of their organizations? This question has not been widely investigated, but emerging research is finding that chairmen fulfill a number of functions that are critical to organizational performance, including leading the board; setting the board's agenda; ensuring that board members receive timely, clear, and accurate information; ensuring the transparency of board processes and discussions; evaluating the performance of the overall board and individual directors; and promoting a constructive relationship between the board and management.

It seems simple enough. But it is not quite what it seems, according to the conclusions of an international survey of boards and chairmen conducted by the United Kingdom's Cranfield School of Management with support from CCL; Manchester Square Partners, a U.K.-based firm that advises senior executives on career development and transition; and Heidrick & Struggles, an Australia-based provider of senior-level executive search and leadership consulting services. The survey discovered that practices of chairmanship and board dynamics differ around the world.

As a result of corporate practices in the United States and the United Kingdom in the 1980s and '90s that were perceived to be corrupt, greater attention to governance disciplines has tightened up board processes, through legislation and voluntary codes

designed to better safeguard the interests of shareholders. Prior to the governance movement, shareholders influenced corporate strategy more through their feet than anything else; they sold their shares rather than exercise their rights as shareholders—to do anything else was simply not worth it. Few shareholders pushed for change. Largely because of this shareholder inaction, the oligarchic, aloof top manager came to the fore—the president and CEO acting without restraint.

In the United Kingdom in the 1990s, CEOs and their top teams were considered the root of corporate excess. The Cadbury Report of 1992 stipulated that the roles of CEO and chairman be separated, with the chairman responsible for leading the board, holding the CEO accountable, and ensuring that the board members have a greater say than formerly in strategy formulation, executive remuneration, and senior appointments. The Cadbury Report transformed the world of the British manager. Today role separation is a reality for 98 percent of U.K.-listed companies. Since Cadbury, separate inquiries have recommended governance improvements, but all of them voluntary. In the United Kingdom today, ultimately the chairman decides what governance to adopt.

The Australians took the British line of role separation and voluntary codes, except that greater pressure to comply is placed on Australian firms by the Australian Stock Exchange and the federal government. In the United States, in contrast, role duality still exists for approximately 76 percent of U.S. listed corporations. The president, the CEO, and the chairman are all the same person. For U.S. corporations, ultimate power is in the hands of these individuals. Setting the board's agenda; determining the quality, quantity, and timing of information presented to the board; and leading the management team are the prerogative of one person. In recent years governance intervention has been through regulation, namely the Sarbanes-Oxley Act of 2002, whereby the president-CEO-chairman and the chief financial officer are legally accountable for transparent, honest, and accurate financial reporting. Research concludes that all other corporate actors help the president-CEO-chairman to achieve his or her goals, in contrast to the British and Australian way of working.

ROLE INFLUENCES
Bearing in mind the divergence of role duality and separation, just how different are the roles of chairmen across the world? The inquiry by Cranfield, CCL, Manchester Square Partners, and Heidrick & Struggles explored the effects of national and regional influences on the roles and contributions of chairmen. Differences of orientation and practice emerged, determined by seven demographics: status, responsibility delineation, vision, recruitment, domicile, role counterbalance, and tenure.

Status
The status of the U.K. and Australian chairmen is high. U.K. chairmen view their appointment as the pinnacle of their careers. The role of chairman opens many doors in British society, facilitating access to government and government appointments despite relatively low remuneration, often 10 to 20 percent of what CEOs earn. However, the honor and prestige more than compensate.

Additionally, U.K. chairmen report little difference in practice between executive and nonexecutive roles. The distinction made is between being full-time or part-time in the job. Irrespective of the individual's number of hours devoted to the job or of the role being executive or nonexecutive, the British chairman's focus is to attend to the duties of the board and, in so doing, to develop a high level of trust with the CEO, monitoring the CEO's performance but allowing him or her to run the show.

The contrast with Australian practice is substantial. More Australian chairmen hold executive responsibilities, often subsuming and downgrading the role of CEO to that of managing director (MD) or just chief operating officer (COO). The Australian chairman runs the company. Certain Australians expressed irritation with what they called the "quaint British thing" of distinguishing between executive and nonexecutive, which they felt were more or less the same thing.

The distinction between executive and nonexecutive also holds little relevance for the U.S. president-CEO-chairman. Having one individual lead both the company and the board is reality for the majority of U.S. companies. In their role of chairman the majority of these leaders say they are attentive to but also critical of Sarbanes-Oxley. Those who view their corporations as promoting the highest standards of governance believe they have implemented the spirit of the legislation, but putting the details of Sarbanes-Oxley into action is expensive. Those who admit to being governance challenged also criticize the legislation. One U.S. independent board director stated, "How can an act of Congress help a board that is overwhelmed (meant *bullied*) by one person when what we need is a strong lead independent director (LID), and that is the last thing our president-CEO-chair will allow?"

The critiques of Sarbanes-Oxley come in two forms. The first is that it is excessive, expensive, and unnecessary; the second is that what is really needed is better leadership, and legislation is not going to help. Other studies have reached similar conclusions. The personality and style of the top leader counts more than anything else. Thus the question remains of which is the best way forward, greater accountability or role separation? To Americans, British role separation slows things down. To the British, Sarbanes-Oxley does not tackle the root of corruption, which is putting power in the hands of one person.

In the U.S. organizations that had separated the president-CEO role and chairman role, the two types of leaders independently reported that the move was a positive step forward and that they had no desire to return to role duality. The checks and balances that come with discussing critical issues improve the quality of decisions. Adjusting to not being totally in charge was considered a problem, but only a temporary one that could be alleviated by good coaching support.

Responsibility Delineation

In Britain chairmen are held accountable for board performance and board decisions. U.S. presidents-CEOs-chairmen and Australian chairmen are held accountable for both board performance and company performance. The only real difference between the Americans and Australians is the legal requirements imposed by Sarbanes-Oxley. However, the Australians have been quick to adopt the tenets of the legislation because of the attraction of trading with the U.S. market.

Among the British chairmen holding executive status, few had any of the traditional line functions reporting directly to them. The British CEO determines the organizational structure that he or she desires and has it ratified by the board. Thus even executive chairmen are more driven by the views of the CEO. The Australians report that the chairman and CEO jointly determine their delineation of responsibilities, although it is plainly evident that the chairman is often the stronger voice.

The most individualistic of the three groups is the U.S. president-CEO-chairman, who unilaterally determines the responsibilities allocated to the roles of chair and CEO. Few of these leaders indicate that they discuss the logic of role allocation with their board members; rather, they simply inform the board of decisions already reached. As the president-CEO-chairman of a U.S. defense contractor stated: "With my future on the line, I will tell you what I do as chairman of the board. I don't need Sarbanes or anyone else to tell me that."

A minority of U.S. chairmen emphasize making time for the members of the board to independently examine issues without the presence of executive management, including themselves in their role of CEO. In effect, the president-CEO-chairman leaves the room so the other board members can continue the debate.

Vision

Driven by role separation, British chairmen admit to being "vision passive." British chairmen challenge, debate, and ultimately sign off on the vision of the CEO and the management team.

In contrast, the proactive Australian chairman often reports outright determination of the vision of the company. Australian chairmen strongly view themselves as the stewards of the vision. The chairman of an Australian financial services company stated: "I am accountable for both the board and the company. I set the vision. Yes, there is a difference between the Australian and British roles of chairman and CEO."

Like Australian chairmen, U.S. chairmen confirm their responsibility for determining and driving forward the vision. However, other board members should raise concerns about this approach. When one person shapes the strategic profile of the enterprise, external or independent board directors can feel inhibited, undermining constructive challenge. Encouraging robust debate requires acting as CEO with the management team and as chairman with the board. The difference is in style, balancing being both assertive and conciliatory and being directive and at the same time listening and influencing. Some U.S. chairmen admit that changing style is not easy. Some report going to great lengths to separately win the support of their management team and the board. One said that in addition to attending board meetings, he visited all board members on their home turf to listen to their concerns and through such personal attention improved board dynamics.

Recruitment

Nationality emerges as a key criterion for the recruitment and appointment of chairmen. In Australia, stringent effort is made to appoint Australians to the role; the purpose is long-term stability. An implicitly held assumption in Australia is that the best executive talent lies overseas, particularly in the United States and the United Kingdom. However, U.S. and U.K. expatriates who remain overseas for longer than five years face substantial tax burdens; therefore their choices are to return home or become Australian citizens.

The chairman of an Australian food manufacturing company stated: "Our top positions are often filled by Americans who after five years go home. I am the anchor. I keep the company together over the long term, so I have to be homegrown and Australian."

For substantially different reasons, a similar consideration is identified in the United States. The U.S. president-CEO-chairman is by nature hands on, driving the business and providing leadership to the board. The president-CEO element of the role—in terms of track record, experience, and management skills—is given priority over the boardroom and chairman capability. Moreover, market considerations dominate board concerns. Therefore it is critical for the president-CEO-chairman to understand the U.S. home markets because "most of our business is over here," as the president-CEO-chairman of a U.S. insurance company stated.

A number of Americans stated that if the role of chairman were to be separated from that of president-CEO, finding suitable candidates for what is a part-time and poorly remunerated job would be problematic. Who would want it?

Of the three groups, it is the British chairmen who display the broadest, most international reach. Proximity to Europe and the United States, the drive for penetration of international markets, and the established practice of role separation position British chairmen to display international understanding. The home market is too small. Thus British chairmen tend to travel more than their U.S. and Australian counterparts. A considerable number of British appointees hold the post of chairman for British, U.S., and continental European companies. Traveling considerable distances to board meetings is viewed as normal, as is accompanying the CEO on international tours—all for a part-time job.

Domicile

An important consideration in the appointment of U.S. and Australian chairmen is the location of the incumbent's home. Australian chairmen, conscious of their executive accountabilities and the need to attend to operational details, report that it is common practice for the chairman to reside in the city where the company is headquartered. Australia is dominated by the twin cities of Melbourne and Sydney, and calling one of these two cities home is important. If potential candidates are not willing to live there, they may as well rule themselves out as applicants for the role.

From the U.S. dual-role perspective the dominance of the president-CEO role requires being geographically close to the headquarters of the firm. However, in the few cases of role separation, domicile and even nationality are of secondary concern as appointment criteria for the role of chairman.

Role Counterbalance

Who challenges the chairman of the board? Practice in the United Kingdom and the United States is similar. Driven by fears of further scandal and that a strong personality could dominate the board and management, companies have introduced an additional board role; in the United States it is the lead independent director (LID) and in the United Kingdom it is the senior independent director (SID). Although it's early to make a full evaluation, the value of the LIDs and SIDs is acknowledged. Cognizant of the danger of groupthink, chairmen and their boards see offering constructive challenge as necessary. However, all admit that this is no easy task, bearing in mind the complexities of boardroom dynamics and the ego of the chairman.

The British report that it is acceptable for the SID to challenge within and outside board meetings. A chairman of a U.K. bank stated, "British nonexecutive directors offer quiet defiance and sort out their affairs before the meeting."

Although similarly configured, LIDs operate differently from SIDs. The greatest level of inhibition across the three groups is identified in American boards. The discomfort in directly challenging the chairman nurtures such an inhibitive atmosphere that a number of board members say their skills and experience are underused. "The chairman knows what he wants and whose skills and experience he wishes to use," said a board member of a U.S. manufacturing company. "Once that is clear, my colleagues and I respect that and do not challenge."

In a similar vein, LIDs do not challenge as much as SIDs but rather tend to work together with the chairman prior to board meetings, determining the agenda and discussing how to address issues, so that by the time of the board meeting the need to challenge is minimized.

The Australian version of the LID or SID is the deputy chairman, but numerous boards report having no such role. Most Australian chairmen report that teamwork is valued at the board level and that any good team has no problem in challenging. But a minority of chairmen and board members report that teamwork is a cover for groupthink. The emerging evidence suggests that Australians are rugged conformists, displaying minimal desire to change.

Tenure

What about staying too long or not long enough on the board? The surprising finding is that constructive and well-handled challenge occurs with greater length of tenure, and it is on this one point that U.S., U.K., and Australian respondents concur. The prevailing governance wisdom is that to stay too long disproportionately increases the individual's chances of becoming corrupted. Well, perhaps for some, but not for the majority, the survey concludes. The longer in the role, the greater the insight into the firm's strengths and weaknesses and the deeper the knowledge and confidence in one another as board members. Some of the fiercest and yet most constructive conversations are reported as taking place between people who have known each other for some time. Length of tenure is reported as correlating with high levels of company performance. British and Australian chairmen report that boards—and companies—that perform above average have members who have been in their roles for eleven to fifteen years. U.S. chairmen and board members confirm the advantage of extended tenure and quote eight to ten years as necessary to make a significant impact.

So much, however, depends on the personality and style of the chairman. The high-performing chairman removes the barriers between people and nurtures a culture of speaking one's mind.

GUIDING THE BOAT

The ancient Greeks defined governance in the form of a person, the *kybernitis*—the helmsman of the boat who guides the vessel through stormy waters. That definition is valuable today. The ancient helmsman adopted particular protocols to help the boat survive the storm, much as today's governance guides the firm through market and performance challenges. What is also important is the leadership style and mind-set of the top man or woman. Just as the Greek helmsman called upon his skill and experience to survive the storm, the integration of leadership with governance makes for outstanding performance.

Yet who is today's *kybernitis*? In the United States, the helmsman is still the president-CEO-chairman. That is not the case in Australia or the United Kingdom, where the chairman and the CEO hold equal or almost equal status and respect.

Leadership today requires displaying outstanding qualities. Given the need for greater understanding of today's global world, it is important for organizations to be cognizant of the substantially different designs for chairmen and boards. Not appreciating the demographic differences that shape the board and key leadership roles leads to unwelcome tension, vulnerability, and risk. Not only does the role of chairman hold different connotations in different parts of the world but also the status, significance, and influence of the role is on the rise.

As organizations are confronted with the complexities of market, shareholder, and governance demands, do not be surprised to find ever greater pressure for role separation in the United States.

Part II

WHY CULTURAL ADAPTABILITY IS IMPORTANT

Bridging Boundaries: Meeting the Challenge of Workplace Diversity

Christopher Ernst and Jeffrey Yip

In today's globally diverse and increasingly interconnected world, social identity boundaries rub together, pull apart, and collide in the workplace. When identity divides open up, people look to leaders to bridge the gaps. By employing four tactics—suspending, reframing, nesting, and weaving— leaders can facilitate positive cross-boundary interactions.

Globalization, rapidly advancing technology, changing demographics, and shifting social structures are creating a modern workplace in which groups of people who have historically remained apart are now working together. This is in turn creating a pressing organizational challenge: the need for leaders to bridge social identity boundaries among groups of people with very different histories, perspectives, values, and cultures. How can organizations best meet this challenge of boundary-spanning leadership?

Boundaries are an unavoidable aspect of organizational life. They can take many forms: they may be functional, geographic, or cultural, and they may be found at the individual, group, or organizational levels. Such boundaries are reinforced through the strong human tendency to categorize people into *in-groups* (people like me) and *out-groups* (people not like me).

In today's globally diverse and increasingly interconnected world, identity boundaries rub together, pull apart, and collide in the workplace. Some of these collisions create minor friction and are quickly resolved; others reveal deep fault lines and significantly affect organizational functioning. Either way, when an identity divide opens up, people look to leaders to bridge the gap.

However, leaders who try to effectively bridge identity divides face at least three major challenges. First, they are often *pulled in various directions* among different identity groups' conflicting

values, viewpoints, and beliefs. Second, they are commo
to one side. A leader will be a member of some identity ~~g~~
not a member of others. Despite a leader's best efforts to ~~be~~ ...
partial and fair, members of identity groups will form perceptions
based solely on his or her identity group membership. And third,
leaders are all too frequently *caught out of the loop.* This occurs in
part because people have a natural tendency to filter information as
it moves up the organizational hierarchy and in part because more
often than not, leaders are representatives of traditionally advantaged and dominant identity groups. Under these circumstances,
leaders often lack critical awareness and knowledge of the inequi-
ties and challenges faced by less advantaged groups.

FINDING LINKS

The role of boundary-spanning leadership is to facilitate cross-
boundary interactions, thereby creating the linkages necessary to
move ideas, information, people, and resources where they are
needed most. Their positional authority allows leaders to establish a number of these linkages *directly* through their actions and
words. At the same time, the three challenges described earlier
impose limitations on this ability of leaders to intervene directly.
As a result, boundary-spanning leaders often act *indirectly,* through
enabling or facilitating the cross-boundary interactions of others.

Four boundary-spanning tactics—*suspending, reframing,
nesting,* and *weaving*—can facilitate positive cross-boundary interactions.

Suspending: Creating a Third Space

The tactic of boundary suspending seeks to create a neutral zone, a third space where social interactions are person based
rather than identity-group based and where individual relationships can be developed, assumptions can be surfaced, personal values can be safely explored, and new language can be created. This
space can be physical (such as an office or other business space),

virtual (such as the communication zone created by e-mailing or teleconferencing), mental (such as the common ground opened by shared experiences, ideas, and ideals), or any combination of these three.

Leadership practices that create a third space can be either formal or informal and can occur as part of work or after-work activities. A human resource director in Singapore cites using sports as a third space to facilitate interaction between Chinese Christian employees and Malay Muslim constituents in the community. These sporting events create a common medium through which ethnic and religious boundaries can be suspended and different identity groups can interact and learn more about each other on an individual level.

Also consider the case of a Japanese project manager whose job required him to work for short stints in countries throughout the Asia-Pacific region. His role demanded that he quickly build productive and task-oriented cross-national teams in order to launch new information technology initiatives. On assignment in Korea, the project manager frequently organized opportunities for his team members from Australia, Indonesia, Korea, and New Zealand to socialize after work, and observed that these interactions were highly effective in developing person-to-person relationships.

Establishing such practices is not always so straightforward, however. In-groups may feel threatened when brought into contact with out-groups with which they have a history of tension or mistrust. An example of this is the Japanese project manager's experience while managing a new initiative in Hong Kong. His efforts to organize after-work activities in this case were met with resistance. Although his expatriate colleagues enjoyed going out to a bar or nightclub to socialize, his local Chinese colleagues preferred to have dinner together. These differences carried over to the workplace. Project delays and behind-the-scenes conversations became the norm. The problem, according to the project manager, was not the technical work but that the different national groups were simply not able to get along.

Bridging entrenched identity divides is something that few leaders have been trained to do, yet it is an integral aspect of their leadership roles. Examples of successful boundary-spanning practices include holding storytelling sessions in which individuals are encouraged to share personal life events and lessons; setting up a *war room* where cross-boundary teams can construct maps, track progress, and have meetings; organizing *creativity labs* where diverse teams can dialogue and solve problems; and arranging off-site retreats designed to take advantage of the third-space qualities of a neutral location.

Reframing: Activating a Shared Identity

The tactic of boundary reframing is designed to activate a common category or superordinate identity that is inclusive across identity groups.

In the workplace, boundary reframing increases the salience, relevance, and importance of belonging to the organization as a higher-level social category. Thus the organization itself and its mission and goals become the all-inclusive identity group.

A powerful example of boundary reframing can be seen at Child Rights and You (CRY), a nonprofit organization in India that has transformed itself from an agency for child relief to an agency for child rights. This grassroots organization spans seventeen of the twenty-eight Indian states and is a microcosm of the tremendous diversity of this vast nation and its intergroup differences in gender, religion, region, language, ethnicity, and caste. Members of the management committee recognized that the transformation would succeed only if all the identity groups within the organization internalized the change.

Bringing the entire organization together in internalizing the transformation helped to discourage an us-versus-them mindset from developing. When regional divisions or rifts between castes become apparent, they can be addressed in the moment rather than externalized. This process allows people to identify common ground and form new levels of trust and community.

The compelling missions of nonprofit organizations can function as built-in superordinate goals with the power to bridge gaps between disparate identity groups. In the corporate setting, superordinate goals tend to focus on achievements such as winning market share, beating the competition, and reaching collective financial targets that result in bonuses or pay raises. These focuses can bridge social identities by emphasizing interorganizational competition and what is positive and distinctive about the organization compared with its competitors.

For example, in a company that manufactures clothing for some of the world's best-known brands, leaders draw on the shared need of employees for financial security. About 40 percent of the employees are Jordanians; the remaining 60 percent are from India, Sri Lanka, Bangladesh, and China. Effectively working together and meeting production targets results in collective financial incentives and rewards; causing trouble and not getting along results in losing your job.

What these examples have in common is the activation of a shared vision. The real boundaries that separate identity groups in these organizations are rooted in group membership and are charged with emotion and meaning. Leaders should not ignore such powerful differences or attempt to make them go away. Nor should they deliberately put members of identity groups in a position where they must abandon core aspects of their social identity in deference to the organizational identity. This practice not only raises ethical issues but also results in an unsustainable strategy.

Nesting: Embedding Groups Within a Larger Whole

The tactic of boundary nesting seeks to structure interactions so that identity groups have distinct roles that are embedded within a larger mission, goal, or objective. It draws on the strong needs humans have for both distinctiveness and belonging.

Common examples of boundary nesting are affinity groups and communities of practice, both of which seek to foster the development of a shared and nested identity while keeping groups connected to a larger organizational identity. Like Russian *matryoshka* dolls, smaller subgroups with unique meaning and integrity are nested within larger groups that constitute the whole. A number of organizations use educational or cultural events to bring social identity groups together.

CRY has adopted an innovative strategy-planning process that uses the concept of boundary nesting. It wanted a strategy process that recognized and valued the distinct regional identities across the organization yet also addressed the need for an integrated long-term plan to provide an overarching blueprint. The outcome is a collective process whereby each region works on the strategy after having broken it down into smaller actionable steps. The final version of the strategy then emerges after the groups cooperate to reconcile their various plans.

A key distinction between boundary suspending and boundary nesting is that in the former, leaders seek to facilitate cross-boundary interactions between individuals, whereas in the latter, they seek to stimulate interactions between groups. Research evidence demonstrates that nesting groups within larger wholes can reduce perceived intergroup threats and anxiety.

Yet nesting can be difficult to put into practice. Given that organizational life is often territorial and status oriented, it is a challenge for leaders to ensure in-group cohesion and at the same time to balance it with cross-group identification with the organization as a whole.

Leaders can manage these tensions by structuring interdependent tasks so that each group's expertise is equally valued. Another option is a tiered approach in which subgroup members first engage in activities that affirm their identity and then the different subgroups are brought together to work toward a shared understanding. Lastly, leaders can deal with these tensions by actively speaking out concerning the unique perspectives brought by various groups and their contributions to larger organizational goals.

In Singapore the nation's first prime minister, Lee Kuan Yew, and subsequent leaders have used these approaches to remarkable effect. Since gaining its independence in 1965, Singapore, a highly multicultural, multiethnic, and multifaith society, has stressed that the nation's strength lies in the diversity of its cultures. The respective ethnic and religious identities are honored for their unique traditions and for their concurrent contributions to the whole of the nation. Such an approach serves to prevent dominant identity groups from asserting their identities above others and protects the unique identities of minority groups.

In Singapore the tactic of boundary nesting has been a powerful force against ethnic discrimination. Its success is evident in the stability of interethnic relations in the country and the ease with which Singaporeans interact with the rest of the world.

Weaving: Cross-Cutting Roles and Identity

The final tactic, boundary weaving, seeks to cross and intersect social and organizational identities in an interdependent manner so that they are less tightly coupled at a limited number of points. Interlacing social identities across various roles and levels in an organization facilitates opportunities for increased cross-boundary collaboration and creativity. Boundary weaving is particularly relevant in bridging the diversity gap between dominant and minority groups in an organization. With the weaving of organizational and social identities, minority-group membership and employment classifications are intersected so that a person's identity is not correlated with his or her employment role or classification.

Boundary-spanning leaders use weaving tactics to facilitate greater representation, opportunity, and voice for identity groups across organizational levels and functions. With the use of modern communication technology, geographically dispersed or virtual teams are an increasingly prevalent mechanism for organizations to use as they seek innovative cross-boundary solutions.

Consider the example of a leader in an Asian multinational organization whose job requires her to implement regional information technology solutions across countries with widely different technology infrastructures. She composes her teams to ensure that their members are mixed in terms of both functional expertise and social identity. What she has learned is that regional diversity is necessary to a deep understanding of end-user norms and values, whereas functional diversity is a valuable way to identify the appropriate technical parameters and solutions. She feels that the cross-boundary composition of her teams is a critical factor in their ability to generate new ideas and depart from conventional solutions.

Global diversity is the new reality of the workplace. For boundary-spanning leaders this diversity is not thought of as a challenge to solve but rather as the very means to solve the challenge. By cross-cutting identity groups with organizational levels and roles, boundary-spanning leaders can unlock the creative potential within individuals and the organization.

RIGHT COMBINATIONS

In practice the four boundary-spanning tactics are closely integrated, as leaders can use different combinations for different situations. This is demonstrated by the example of Ong Keng Yong, former secretary-general of the Association of Southeast Asian Nations (ASEAN).

Comprising Brunei, Cambodia, Indonesia, Laos, Malaysia, Myanmar, the Philippines, Singapore, Thailand, and Vietnam, ASEAN is an association of nation-states that have vastly differing economic and political statuses and are home to more than 500 million people. The leadership challenge and opportunity faced by Ong was in working across the various cultural and political differences represented in ASEAN while moving the group toward regional integration.

Ong described ASEAN meetings as forums where boundaries of national identities were *suspended* and representatives of member states engaged in person-to-person dialogue on issues of shared interest. In these settings he *reframed* intergroup differences by actively staking out the common ground. *Nesting* was seen in the secretary-general's efforts to uphold the distinct traditions of member nations; during ASEAN meetings Ong ensured that member states were given opportunities to contribute their unique knowledge and experience toward ASEAN goals and objectives. Lastly, as a political association ASEAN was noteworthy in its use of *weaving,* exemplified in the diverse representation and rotation of member states across levels and roles.

As this example of boundary-spanning leadership illustrates, if people of different identity groups are provided with opportunities for positive cross-boundary contact in the workplace, then these experiences can spill over into local communities. Boundary-spanning leadership has the potential to transform long-standing biases and beliefs. The impact is felt not only within the individual organization but also in the broader community or society. Through the work of boundary-spanning leaders, organizations can act as levers for positive societal change.

Cultural Intelligence and the Global Economy

Joo-Seng Tan

Among the skills required to be a successful global leader is cultural intelligence—the ability to adapt to new cultural settings. Cultural intelligence has three key parts: thinking and solving problems in particular ways, being energized and persistent in one's actions, and acting in certain ways. Today more and more organizations and individuals are seeing cultural intelligence as a competitive advantage and strategic capability.

Among the twenty-first-century skills that are frequently talked about are the ability to adapt constantly to different people from diverse cultures and the ability to manage the interconnectedness of today's world. The global workplace requires individuals to be sensitive to different cultures, to interact appropriately with people from different cultures, and to analyze new cultures as they are encountered. To do all this, individuals, whether they are at home or abroad, need cultural intelligence. It is needed to manage the stress of culture shock and the consequent frustration and confusion that typically result from clashes of cultural differences. It is essential to facilitating effective cross-cultural adjustment.

Positioning cultural intelligence as a key concept in the global economy raises several questions that concern both individuals and organizations:

- How do individuals develop their capability to adapt effectively across different cultures?
- Why do some individuals possess superior capacity to deal with the challenges of working in different cultures?

- How do individuals reach full productive potential working in culturally diverse work environments in their home countries and overseas?

- How do organizations build capability for effective work assignments in locations around the world?

- How do organizations optimize individual and collective performance when they harness the cultural diversity of their people across the world?

In *CQ: Developing Cultural Intelligence at Work* (Stanford Business Books, 2006), coauthors P. Christopher Earley (dean and James Brooke Henderson Professor of Management at Purdue University's Krannert School of Management), Soon Ang (executive director of the Center for Innovation Research in Cultural Intelligence and Leadership in Singapore), and I tackle these questions by explaining what cultural intelligence is and showing how cultural intelligence is applied in the workplace.

MAKING ADJUSTMENTS

We suggest that one way to understand cultural intelligence is in relation to emotional or social intelligence. Emotional intelligence presumes that people are familiar with their own culture and that they (often unconsciously) use familiar situations as a way to interact with others. Cultural intelligence picks up where emotional intelligence leaves off—it involves dealing with people and situations in unfamiliar surroundings.

Cultural intelligence determines a person's ability to adjust to new cultures. Thus cultural intelligence can be defined as a person's ability to successfully adapt to new cultural settings—that is, to unfamiliar settings attributable to cultural context.

Cultural intelligence has three key parts: thinking and solving problems in particular ways (*cultural strategic thinking*), being energized and persistent in one's actions (*motivational*), and acting in certain ways (*behavioral*).

Cultural strategic thinking refers partly to the general thinking skills that an individual uses to create an understanding of how and why people in a culture new to that individual act as they do. This understanding captures not just what the people believe or value but also the procedures and routines that they are supposed to use as they work and act. The ideas that we have about what people in a new culture believe or value are called *declarative knowledge,* or knowledge about the state of things. For example, if I know that in Bali children are named according to their birth order, this is declarative knowledge (knowledge of facts). However, if I know that in China one empties one's glass after a toast (*gan bei*), this is knowledge of procedures, or *procedural knowledge.* Thus cultural knowledge encompasses both the facts that we hold about another culture and our knowledge of how things operate. In addition to cultural knowledge, cultural strategic thinking involves cultural thinking and learning—that is, the process through which we gain our cultural knowledge. This kind of cultural thinking and learning, called metacognition by psychologists, has also been referred to as *thinking about thinking* or *learning to learn.* These two elements work together; cultural strategic thinking guides the strategies that people use to acquire knowledge about country-specific information. Clearly, cultural thinking and learning and acquiring cultural knowledge are both critical to success.

Creating a way to make sense of new and radically different situations is an important task in developing cultural intelligence. Culturally intelligent managers aren't just learning the ways that people act and behave in a new place. They are also creating a new mental framework for understanding what they experience and see. That is why cultural strategic thinking is also what psychologists call *higher-order thinking;* it refers to *how* we learn, not just *what* we learn. In contrast, in applying approaches such as emotional or social intelligence, people use their existing knowledge of how things function in their culture to decide how and when to act in any particular situation.

GETTING MOTIVATED

Personal knowledge alone, however, isn't enough. Certain actions not within a person's current repertoire may be needed for an appropriate response in a new culture. Simple examples abound in the anecdotes of international managers, which tell of everything from discovering the proper way to shake someone's hand in Ghana (involving a finger click at the end of the handshake) to learning to eat exotic local delicacies without showing hesitation or disgust.

The difficulty is that many of these actions are easily overlooked yet they have a cumulative impact on the quality of our interactions with others. One manager from Canada relayed the story of meeting a group of managers from a Mexican joint venture. He noticed after several minutes of talking with his Mexican counterpart that they had moved around the meeting room as if engaged in a dance. He later realized that as they spoke, the Mexican manager would draw closer. As he did so, the Canadian manager would unconsciously draw back. The two managers were acting like two magnets with a common charge.

So without proper motivation, you won't adjust. If a person is unmotivated and won't engage the world, why should we expect to find successful adaptation? Here, for example, is what one Korean manager said of his experiences on a multinational team:

> *They were trying not to listen to me. Sometimes they were changing the topic after my speaking. They were not paying attention. It went on like this for at least one or two months, and this was a bad experience. Later I just gave up trying to speak.*

This manager was able to understand what was going on and why, but he was not motivated to try to deal with the cultural situation. His attitude reflected his own low motivation and lack of confidence in his ability to work effectively, so he disengaged from his team. Cultural intelligence means knowing *and* trying.

ACTION PLAN

The final piece of cultural intelligence is a person's ability to *do the right thing,* to engage in action that is adaptive. An unfortunate oversight in most of the current work on intelligence is that an action component is often neglected. I suppose this occurs because psychologists often pigeonhole their work, seeing it as belonging to either cognitive psychology or behavioral psychology, each type having its own independent supporters. From a management perspective, it seems to me woefully shortsighted to separate what people think from what they do. Ultimately, business requires action, not simply intention. Similarly, cultural intelligence is not stagnant when it comes to behavior. A person's actions are dynamic and must adjust to the changing nature of the work environment. It's not enough to have a *potential* for action; potential realized through one's actions partly determines cultural intelligence.

To summarize, cultural intelligence reflects an intersection of three paths—thinking about a new culture (the individual has direction), being motivated and feeling confident to act (the individual is energized), and creating the actions needed for the situation (the individual is adaptive).

To me, cultural intelligence isn't meaningful unless it means that actions are completed. As we know from popular folklore, deeds are worth a great deal more than intentions, and that is why cultural intelligence must involve the ability to carry out the actions needed in a particular culture. Without appropriate action, a person may know what to do and feel motivated to act, but it will all be for naught.

CORPORATE MODELS

Today more organizations and individuals see cultural intelligence as a competitive advantage and strategic capability. In this section I present evidence that various corporations already possess an orientation toward cultural intelligence, are enjoying the benefits of hiring individuals who are culturally intelligent, and have cultural intelligence as a core part of their corporate strategy.

IBM firmly believes that cross-cultural competence is the glue that enables cohesiveness and collective performance. In the high-performance environment of the global marketplace, cultural intelligence is a strategic capability of leaders and managers. Organizations and individuals who see the strategic value of cultural intelligence are able to effectively leverage cultural differences for competitive advantage and achieve competitive superiority in the global marketplace.

In the global scramble for talent, organizations aspire to be the employer of choice. They hope to attract, develop, and retain the best talent in their organizations. Organizations such as Novartis and Nike see the competitive advantage of hiring individuals who are culturally intelligent. These organizations also adopt cultural diversity as an integral part of their human resource agenda. They identify focus areas for cultural diversity and link cultural diversity and the HR business case.

Culturally intelligent individuals who can respond effectively to customers from different cultures are also welcomed at Lloyds TSB. In fact, Lloyds TSB takes the challenge of improving customer relationships so seriously that it has a diversity strategy to deal with it. The strategy has contributed to increased income streams and better cost management.

Culturally intelligent individuals who are able to leverage cultural diversity to align marketing and product development with consumers can provide a competitive edge in product development and marketing strategies for consumer groups in different countries. Levi Strauss capitalizes on this strategy to grow its business globally.

Lufthansa believes that culturally intelligent individuals constitute a precious organizational asset during times of crisis. At Barclays, culturally intelligent individuals will help the organization gain local ownership and commitment in the

United Kingdom and beyond. As suggested by Lynn Offerman, a professor of industrial and organizational psychology at George Washington University, individuals' ability to work and adapt in an environment where assumptions, values, and traditions differ from those they are accustomed to reflects cultural intelligence. This adjustment requires skills and abilities very different from those that individuals might use in familiar surroundings.

It is evident that organizations leverage culturally intelligent individuals to achieve organizational goals and strategies. Individuals who are culturally intelligent provide a source of competitive advantage for multinational companies. From a leadership perspective, culturally intelligent leaders can improve the cooperation of employees from different countries and cultures.

Cultural Adaptability: It's About More Than Using the Right Fork

Maxine A. Dalton

For global managers, adapting to the cultures of the countries in which they conduct business is a crucial capability. It's also an often misunderstood capability, one that can easily be diminished through oversimplification. As global managers work at adapting to other cultures, they need to be mindful of issues of appropriateness and ethics.

Managers in global organizations know all about getting advice. One piece of guidance that they're offered repeatedly—by their bosses, researchers, consultants, coaches, books, and newspaper and magazine articles—is that they need to be able to adapt their thinking and behavior to the cultures in which they work. They're told to read books and take classes that will teach them about the customs and business practices in other countries. They're counseled to learn a second or even a third language. And they're directed to develop a global mind-set and look to the intersections of countries and cultures for opportunities to create new products and services.

It's all good advice. In fact, global managers who don't follow it are less likely to be successful in their international business endeavors. And yet global managers also need to realize that cultural adaptability is not an absolute—that in certain circumstances it can raise issues of appropriateness and even ethics.

Cultural adaptability ranges from the simple and everyday—such as knowing and following the table manners used in a particular culture—to the complex and profound—such as considering and abiding by a culture's most basic values and beliefs.

It is at the higher end of this spectrum that global managers must employ their knowledge and especially their judgment to sort out complicated cultural signals and personal and business dilemmas, then take the right actions at the right times. Failing to do so can cause global managers' best-intentioned efforts to backfire. Consider the following three examples, all based on stories from the business pages of U.S. newspapers:

- *Ben is the human resource director of a U.S.-based technology manufacturing company that has operations in a number of countries. The company recently opened a factory in Malaysia, and Ben is convinced that the nation's young women, who typically have small hands and good manual dexterity, make excellent workers for the factory's assembly line.*

In an effort to recruit, motivate, and retai
employees, Ben persuades the company to install ʼ
teller machines in the plant. His aim is to create
tive for the women by allowing them access to the money
they earn, giving them newfound independence. But Ben has
disregarded a long-standing national custom that requires
young women to turn over their paychecks to their fathers or
husbands. Rather than acknowledging the potency of this aspect of Malaysian culture and adapting to it, Ben has rashly
imposed the customs of his home country.

He was concerned only with the goal of getting and
keeping his preferred workforce and forgot to look at the big
picture. In doing so he infringed on a culture's centuries-old
familial and social relationships and obligations, raising the
resentment of a male population on whose goodwill his company depends to maintain smooth operations. And Ben is not
the only one at fault; other company managers should also
have been more diligent in gathering and applying knowledge
of the Malaysian culture.

• Activists in the United States and Great Britain are trying to
organize a consumer boycott of chocolate made from African
cocoa beans, responding to reports that the workers who pick
the beans do so under abysmal conditions.

Upon investigation, however, several newspapers find
that the bean pickers' working conditions are typical of, or
in many cases better than, those of other types of workers in
the region. Judging by Western standards, the bean pickers'
working conditions are admittedly dismal, but the workers
themselves say they don't feel mistreated and believe they're
lucky to have employment.

Should the global managers of the Western companies that harvest the beans be guided by the standards of the
region—and thus risk selling fewer candy bars and putting
people out of work because of the boycott—or do they have a

responsibility to improve the bean pickers' working conditions beyond those that are representative of the area?

- *Under pressure from college students who threaten to boycott U.S.-based companies whose products are believed to be made in foreign sweatshops, a major clothing retailer demands that a Mexican factory it uses improve conditions for workers. Mexican labor organizers opposed to the government-controlled unions seize on this action as a sign of international support, the population rallies behind them, and the stability of the new Mexican president's administration is threatened.*

  Do companies have the right to make decisions that could have far-reaching effects on the internal politics of foreign countries, or should they always avoid meddling in the affairs of other nations and honor the traditional ways of doing business?

These examples make it clear that cultural adaptability involves far more than knowing which fork to use, how to present your business card to clients in Asia, or even when and how to change your management style. Cultural adaptability must arise from a far deeper and broader understanding of other cultures, and two things are required to achieve that perceptiveness. First, global managers should be keenly aware of all the ramifications of the cultural adaptations they make or don't make. Second, they must know when to limit both accommodations to other cultures and the imposition of their own culture's values on other cultures.

FIGURE IT OUT

Global managers almost need to become anthropologists. They should develop a strategy for noticing how things are done in other cultures and why. When people observe people from other cultures behaving in ways that are difficult to comprehend, they typically respond in one of three ways—they attack, retreat, or try to figure it out. Global managers have a mandate to take the third option—and they can approach that option best by paying attention, gathering information, and suspending judgment.

One of the best roadmaps for global managers who seek to ground themselves in the cultural norms of other countries has come from social psychologist Shalom Schwartz. "The study of cultural values represents an attempt to identify how the ecology, geography, topography, language, religion, and socio-historical and political context of a given region of the world have interacted to create a recognizable cultural template or prototype of human values that are relatively homogeneous within a region or country," he wrote in his chapter of the 1992 volume of the series *Advances in Experimental Social Psychology*. Later, in a 1995 article in the *Journal of Cross-Cultural Psychology*, Schwartz and coauthor Lilach Sagiv wrote that "cultural value priorities influence how social resources (human capital, money, land) are invested and . . . how organizational performance is evaluated. At the broadest level, cultural value priorities are used to guide and to justify the public policy decisions of nations."

READING UP

A good way for global managers to begin gaining a deeper understanding of a culture's value priorities is by reading books about the region in which the culture lies. The subject matter can be whatever most interests you—geography, religion, history, biography, politics, philosophy, or sociology—and the genre can be nonfiction, fiction, or even poetry. All of these can provide insights into how people in a particular region or country came to think, believe, and act as they do.

Becoming immersed in a country's music, cinema, theater, artwork, cuisine, sports, and even its comic books can also teach global managers a great deal about how people live; which relationships they value and how they structure those relationships;

Finding Help on Tough Issues

In weighing cultural issues and ethical principles when making difficult business decisions, global managers don't have to go it alone. A number of organizations have developed resources that can steer managers in their international business dealings.

- The Caux Round Table, a group of senior business leaders from around the world, has developed a set of principles for business.

  Founded in 1986 in response to rising trade tensions, the Caux Round Table promotes corporate and individual responsibility as a way to reduce social and economic threats to world peace and stability. Starting from the premise that business behavior affects relationships among nations and the prosperity and well-being of their peoples, the principles for business offer guidelines on topics such as the responsibilities of businesses, following international and domestic rules, and respect for the environment.

  According to the Caux Round Table, the principles are rooted in two basic ethical ideals: human dignity and the Japanese concept of *kyosei*. Human dignity refers to the sacredness or value of each person as an end rather than simply a means to the fulfillment of the purposes of others. *Kyosei* means living and working together for the common good, enabling cooperation and mutual prosperity to coexist with healthy and fair competition.

  The principles have been published on the web in eleven languages; they can be found at www.cauxround-table.org.

- The World Business Council for Sustainable Development is a coalition of 150 international companies committed to economic growth, ecological balance, and social progress. The Geneva-based organization's Web site, at www.wbcsd.org, includes information on the group's views and activities in the areas of business leadership, policy development, best practices, and global outreach, as well as case studies of international companies that have improved their bottom lines while also successfully addressing social and environmental issues.

- The United Nations' Universal Declaration of Human Rights, although it addresses fundamental issues that go beyond business concerns, is a useful template for global managers striving to conduct business ethically. Adopted by the General Assembly in 1948, the declaration is available at www.un.org/en/documents/udhr.

- The Chicago-based Council for a Parliament of the World's Religions believes that the world's religions hold a common set of core values that form the basis for a global ethic. For more information, e-mail info@parliamentofreligions.org or call 312/629-2990.

their views on friendship, cooperation, and competition; whom they consider heroes and villains, and why; and the role of work in their lives.

Reading the local English-language newspapers can also yield a trove of information useful in discerning a culture. Take notice of the kinds of issues covered most prominently (or hardly at all) and how they are presented, and how the relationships among the government, unions, banks, schools, and religions are portrayed. Doing so can help global managers recognize the norms that govern, reward, and sanction the beliefs and values of a country's citizens—some of whom are the global managers' colleagues, employees, customers, and vendors.

RIGHT AND WRONG

For global managers, deciding when it is appropriate, wise, and strategically sound to adapt to local customs and when it might be better to follow the practices and values of their own countries or organizations can be a tricky business. Such decisions are more likely to be made correctly when they are based on the deep cultural understanding described previously. And there are other guidelines as well.

First, global managers should consult their own sense of ethics. If a proposed action just feels right or wrong, managers need to pay attention to those instincts. It's often helpful for a global manager to talk the issue over with someone he or she trusts—perhaps a friend, colleague, or spouse—to sort out right from wrong. If attempting to adapt to a culture or impose your own culture entails violating your own strongly held sense of ethics, it's usually a recipe for disaster.

Second, global managers should learn and follow their company policies for ethical conduct in other cultures. If the company has no such policies, global managers should lobby to get some developed, approved, and put into writing. It's not fair or good business sense to expect global managers to make critical ethical and strategic decisions in a vacuum and on the fly.

Third, global managers can consult standards of ethics and human rights and behavior that have been developed by several international organizations. Global managers might also want to have their companies explore membership in one of these organizations.

DOMINO EFFECT

In any discussion of cultural adaptability, one of the key questions is, How much is too much? As globalization has come of age, concern has been raised about its potential negative effects, such as homogenization, a blurring of national and cultural identities, and loss of local control. It has become increasingly evident that to be effective and to resist these negative effects, global managers must have a thorough knowledge of and acute insight into cultural issues. They can no longer attend exclusively to the interests of their own organizations, because doing so can come back to haunt them. Their decisions and actions affect the well-being of people in other cultures and the internal workings of other countries, so they have a responsibility to predict and understand the consequences of those decisions and actions and to revisit, renew, and revise their positions over time.

One Prescription for Working Across Cultures

Craig Chappelow

Leaders who travel around the world often must do so on short notice and have little time to prepare for every possible subtle cultural difference they may encounter. Here are some anecdotes about key events the author experienced in his travels—some elementary and many embarrassing, but all educational.

For me, the best part of working in the field of leadership and leadership development has been the opportunity to travel to other countries to work with clients. As much as I would like to prepare for every possible subtle cultural difference I encounter, however, the reality is that I travel on short notice. So I have adopted a simple dictum that I apply when I'm visiting and working in other countries. It's stolen from the medical profession: *First, do no harm.* It boils down to using basic manners and a bit of self-awareness to monitor my behavior—for instance, whether I'm being too loud or hogging people's personal space. (Both are my tendencies.)

There are a number of resources that I use to get a quick overview of the basic do's and don'ts in encounters with other cultures. I particularly like the *Culture Shock!* series of books from Graphic Arts Center Publishing Company; they teach me just enough to not offend. For anyone considering spending time in France, I enthusiastically recommend Polly Platt's *French or Foe? Getting the Most Out of Visiting, Living, and Working in France* (Distribooks, 2003, third edition), in which you learn, among other things, why *not* to smile at a French shopkeeper.

But very little of our important learning comes from reading books. Most significant learning results from experiencing key events (which in my case generally means screwing things up). I try to gain as much knowledge as I can from such events and to never repeat a mistake. Here's a look at some of the key events I have experienced in my travels—some were elementary and many were embarrassing, but all were educational.

WATCH WHAT YOU EAT

Table manners vary wildly from place to place, and you'll often encounter some quirky edibles. At a dinner party in Australia, one of the dessert courses was a rectangular piece of nougat. After unwrapping the outer foil, I discovered a second, thinner layer of white paper covering the candy.

I painstakingly removed each bit of the paper, even though it was disintegrating in my fingers. Finally my host said, "G'wan, Craig, eat the paper. It's made of rice." I looked up to see that I was the only one at the table with a neat pile of crispy pieces of paper next to my plate.

TRADITIONAL APPROACH

Taking a genuine interest in other people's heritage can go a long way. I once asked a Saudi businessman if there were still Bedouins in his country. I remembered reading about them in Leon Uris's book *The Haj*, and I was intrigued by the idea of twenty-first-century nomads. The businessman was surprised but pleased when I asked. It turned out he was descended from a Bedouin family, and he proceeded to happily tell me stories about his family's tribe.

EAGER TO PLEASE

One benefit of traveling is that I have learned to extend to visitors to the United States the same hospitality I have received around the world.

During a trip to New Zealand, a co-worker and I stopped at a store to ask for directions to a tourist attraction in a distant town. The woman in the store immediately called a relative in the town to get directions. Later my colleague and I got off track and stopped to ask a farmer for directions. He insisted that we come into his barn to see his newborn calves.

That night we were still driving way out in the country, and by that time we were starving. We managed to find a restaurant, only to discover it was closed for the night. But the maitre d' unlocked the door and let us in. The cook had gone home, but the maitre d' went into the kitchen and emerged a few minutes later with a giant bowl of French fries and garlic bread. He said it was the only thing he knew how to cook. To us it was ambrosia.

RIDING SHOTGUN

On my first visit to Australia I jumped in the back seat of an airport taxi. I told the cabby where I wanted to go but he just sat there, looking at me in the rearview mirror. Finally he said, "Well, are you going to come ride up front or just sit in back like an American?" I was a little puzzled (not to mention jet-lagged) but moved to the front seat.

STEER CLEAR

I've noticed that there are wide variations among cultures in people's need for personal space. The English, for instance, tend to need a lot of it. One of the funniest scenes in the movie *The Full Monty* is the one in which the jobless steelworkers pulsate to a disco beat in the unemployment line. Even as they break into spontaneous dance, each one maintains an invisible but precise bubble of space around himself. I've learned that when I get on an elevator in London and everyone backs away, it isn't a reflection on my hygiene.

KEEP MOVING

In a remote public market in the Guatemalan highlands, I found myself packed in among hundreds of locals shouldering their way through the narrow rows between the stalls, where everything from cornmeal to kittens was for sale. When I slowed down a little to look more closely at something, I felt myself being propelled forward by a hand in the small of my back. Behind me a tiny woman was politely but firmly keeping me moving through the crowd. I noticed this was a frequent practice among the locals.

BAD HAIR DAY

I awoke early in my hotel in Shanghai, with an entire Sunday to do as I pleased. My body was still on U.S. time, and I was wide-awake at 4 a.m. At 6 I decided to take a walk and find some breakfast. Even though it was early, the streets were already crowded. I stopped to rest and watched a surreal scene: white-clad senior citizens doing aerobics to big-band music. As I sat on the edge of a concrete planter, an ancient man came and plopped down right next to me, so close that our legs were touching. He knew a little English and struck up a conversation. Another man came and sat on my other side. He began rubbing his hand up and down my arm, laughing. As I recoiled he pointed at the hair on my arm and then at his arm, which was hairless. I felt a little as though I belonged in the primate house.

ACCIDENTAL CHEAPSKATE

One thing I always do before going to a new country is to familiarize myself with the currency and the exchange rate. One time at a gift shop in Ireland, I was behind an American couple who apparently hadn't bothered to do so. They were holding up the line as they engaged in a loud conversation about the difficulties of keeping track of *foreign* money.

MESSING WITH TEXAS

During a dinner in France with a dozen European participants in a leadership development program, the conversation turned to President George W. Bush, who was new on the job. The Europeans immediately launched into jokes about Bush, most of which ridiculed his intellectual capacity. At first I took offense, thinking they were ganging up on me. But soon I was cracking up along with them. The jokes weren't all that funny, but it's hard not to laugh when you hear French, German, and Italian versions of a Texas accent. Later, one of the participants gave me something of a compliment when he told me I wasn't too uptight—for an American.

I like to think that these and similar experiences have widened my awareness of other cultures to the extent that I really am doing no harm. My ultimate goal is to gain a deeper understanding and acceptance of the nuances of a few specific cultures. Just don't walk up behind me and rub my arm.

Getting the Message: How to Feel Your Way with Other Cultures

Don W. Prince and Michael H. Hoppe

When leaders work and conduct business with people of other cultures, their cultural biases can emerge with force. They need to expect that cultural differences will surface, recognize those differences by the discomfort they produce, and anticipate that those differences will create a need for more thoughtful and deliberate communication.

During a visit to a foreign country, distant city, or even another company, cultural differences can seem colorful, exotic, and appealing. But when the time spent in another culture is longer than a visit, or when you work and conduct business with people of other cultures, your cultural biases can emerge with more force. The disregard for time that seemed so delightful on the island vacation feels very different on Monday morning in the office when the clock is ticking. A modest, deferential manner that was appealing in one cultural context may strike you as passive and ineffectual in a conference room.

These experiences feel unfamiliar because we are looking through the lens of our own cultural expectations. Unconsciously we expect other people to think, feel, and act the way we do. When they don't conform to our expectations, we put our own interpretations on their behavior. But when you're working across cultures, interpretation often becomes misinterpretation. You run the risk of negatively judging the words and actions of people of other cultures or incorrectly assigning motives to unfamiliar behavior because you're viewing an experience from the limited perspective of your own culture.

The discomfort you feel when cultural boundaries collide can be used to your benefit by alerting you to cultural differences. In your interactions with other people, be aware that cultural differences may be coming into play when you experience feelings such as confusion, anxiety, frustration, misunderstanding, tension, impatience, irritation, or anger.

FEET ON THE GROUND

When you feel uncomfortable, it's natural to retreat from that discomfort. After all, you probably feel you are most effective as a manager when you are operating from a familiar place, where you can draw confidence from and make decisions based on past experience. From our work at CCL, we have coined the phrase *jump-back response* to describe this desire to retreat. To be more effective when communicating across cultures, resist your jump-back response. Stay with the uncomfortable experience and learn from it. Compare the unexpected and discomforting behaviors you experience when communicating across cultures against your knowledge of your cultural expectations.

Why doesn't she just say yes or no? In one culture an indirect answer may signal indecisiveness, whereas in another culture it may signal deference and respect.

Why is he always staring at me like that? In one culture staring may signal aggressiveness or intimidation, whereas in another culture direct eye contact may show attention and esteem.

Why does he have to get right in my face whenever he talks to me? In one culture the halo of personal space and privacy may be much smaller than it is in another culture.

Why doesn't she tell me if she doesn't understand something? In one culture asking questions may be accepted as an effective tool for communications, but in another culture questioning superiors may signal insolence.

Why does he sit there smiling when I'm talking about his performance problems? In one culture smiling during a discussion about performance problems may signal contempt and disinterest, whereas in another culture a smile may reflect sincerity and attention.

Why does he make a joke out of everything? In one culture a glib nature may signal a lack of confidence or seriousness, but in another culture it may be a sign of deference.

Change Your Style?

When you work with people of other cultures, you should expect that differences will surface, recognize those cultural differences by the discomfort they produce, and anticipate that those differences will create a need for more thoughtful and deliberate communication. Don't assume that your own cultural customs are correct and superior to others or take the attitude that the other person has to change his or her ways. Be alert to the need to modify your communication style when

- another person's behavior makes you uncomfortable.

- another person's response or reaction seems inappropriate or confusing.

- you assume that you're right and the other person is wrong.

- you stereotype and denigrate another cultural group.

- you ignore or exclude someone because understanding, and making yourself understood, seems too difficult.

It's important to make changes in your communication patterns quickly once you recognize that changes are necessary. A person from another culture is likely to be forgiving the first and second times you make a mistake, but if you persist you will appear ignorant, insensitive, dismissive, or disrespectful.

Consider, for example, the use of *why* questions as a way to get more information. In some cultures, such as that of the United States, it's completely acceptable to ask, "Why did you do the job this way?" In other cultures, Japan's, for example, the same question is considered rude because it puts the other person on the defensive. In this case you can change your communication behavior: "That's an interesting approach you took to the problem. Tell me a little more about it." This gives the other person a chance to share more information with you without risk. Other simple changes that you can make after recognizing different cultural behaviors include learning how to make the correct greeting (a handshake? a bow? a hug?), when to offer your business card (before or after the other person does?), and when and how to question superiors.

NOT SO EASY

When you listen to people who have the same cultural background and native language as you do, you can usually get the gist of their meaning without special effort. You can easily understand their words and "read" their body language and tone of voice. You can make assumptions that are valuable shortcuts to understanding.

When you listen to people from other cultures, your task is more difficult. You can't make the same assumptions. Effective cross-cultural communication requires an extra measure of awareness and attention. To focus on the other person's message, keep the following questions in mind each time you communicate across cultures:

- What do I know about this person's culture?
- Do I take the time to focus on a person from another culture, so I can understand where he or she is "coming from"?
- Do I pay attention to a person's words and body language?
- Do I listen for feelings and unvoiced questions?
- Do I clarify and confirm what I have heard?
- Do I check to make sure the other person has fully understood what I said?

NONVERBAL COMMUNICATION

Whether you're talking to someone from your own culture or someone with a different cultural perspective, much of the message is relayed through nonverbal cues. When communicating across cultures, it's important not only to hear what the other person is saying but also to observe what that person's body language (facial expressions, hand gestures, eye contact, tone of voice) is saying.

Keep in mind, however, that like spoken language, nonverbal expressions such as eye contact and body position have different meanings in different cultures. A clenched fist, a slouched posture, an open hand, or a smile can tell us how to understand a communication only if we have a cultural context for defining the body language.

Even silence can communicate. In some cultures, remaining silent after someone has spoken shows respectful contemplation and consideration of the person's words. If your culture doesn't allow for such conversational pauses, resist filling these gaps with additional explanations and alternative wording.

Also remember that body language is a two-way medium—your own gestures and facial expressions can have unintended messages when you are communicating with someone from another culture. Although your words may say otherwise, your body can communicate boredom, defiance, persuasion, or condescension.

How can you interpret, or "hear," all of that body language if you're not familiar with the other culture? Keep your eyes open for patterns of behavior among various cultural groups. Ask a trusted person from the cultural group. Read up on the business customs of other cultures, and pull information from the Internet (travel sites can be especially helpful in describing cultural customs).

SELF-REFLECTION HELPS

Another good place to start is with a look at your own body language. Ask someone to videotape a presentation that you give at your organization, or observe yourself in a mirror. Ask yourself:

- What do my nonverbal communications look like?

- How might I be perceived by someone with a different cultural background?

- Do I match the stereotype of people from my country?

- How can I check if I suspect that my body language is being misinterpreted by someone from another culture?

Body language is not a universal language. If you experience unexpected behavior when you are trying to communicate in a cross-cultural setting, it's likely that the other person's culture is different from yours and that you are unfamiliar with the cultural context behind the behavior. Consider the following scenarios:

A manager is conducting an annual performance review with one of his direct reports. He begins the session by discussing all the areas in which the employee's performance met or exceeded goals. The employee listens attentively, with a serious and thoughtful expression. But when the manager begins to discuss weaknesses and problem areas, the employee starts smiling. The sterner the manager's tone, the broader the employee grins. The employee doesn't comment on anything the manager says or defend or explain himself. The manager becomes angry because he believes the employee is mocking him and treating the evaluation as a joke.

Sustained eye contact means respect and attentiveness in some cultures but is a rude invasion of privacy in others. A gesture that denotes enthusiastic approval in some cultures is an insult in others. In this case the employee's smile was not a sign of mockery but an expression of deep embarrassment and shame. The manager's angry feelings toward the employee's behavior signal that there may be a miscommunication because of cultural differences.

Frank and Nick leave the office to go to lunch together. When they get into the elevator, Nick stands one foot away from Frank even though the elevator is otherwise empty. When Frank moves a couple of steps away, Nick moves closer to him so that they are almost touching.

Every culture has its own standards about how much personal space feels right and comfortable. From Frank's cultural perspective, physical closeness is an expression of intimacy and feels completely inappropriate in a business relationship. In Nick's cultural view, such closeness is natural behavior. Putting more distance between himself and Frank would show that they don't know or don't like each other.

John goes to the airport to meet Yuri's plane. The two men have talked several times on the phone but have met only once before. When Yuri spots John in the baggage area, he enthusiastically embraces him and kisses him on both cheeks. John feels uncomfortable and hopes nobody he knows has witnessed this greeting.

Every culture has its own unwritten rules about touching. In John's culture the only acceptable touching in business relationships is a handshake. In Yuri's culture bear hugs and kisses are an acceptable and even expected form of greeting, no matter what the relationship is and regardless of gender.

When Hong Mei presents her proposal at the meeting, Vincent reacts strongly. He pounds on the table and questions her in a loud voice. When Hong Mei casts her eyes down in embarrassment, Vincent seems to get more excited. He leans across the table and jabs his hand toward her face.

Every culture has its own ideas about what kind of emotional expression is acceptable and right. In Hong Mei's culture, emotional reserve and restraint are cherished and expected. In Vincent's culture feelings are freely expressed in loud voices, expansive gestures, grimaces, groans, and exclamations. Anything less conveys coldness and disengagement.

Susan travels to London for a meeting with Gillian and Philip. She wants to make a good impression and to indicate that she is happy to be working with them, so she nods and smiles at their comments and observations.

Even the most innocent gestures can be misconstrued. Susan thinks her smiles and nods indicate attentiveness and express her happiness at being part of the team. Gillian and Philip come from a cultural background in which attentiveness and sincerity are marked by a reserved demeanor. Susan's behavior indicates to them that she is insincere, superficial, and unprofessional.

Just as spoken words can be misunderstood during a cross-cultural encounter, so too can nonverbal behavior. If a behavior upsets you beyond what seems appropriate, that's a good sign that cultures are colliding, not communicating. Ask questions to make sure you understand the meaning of behavior that seems out of place.

NEW WORLD, NEW LENSES

Managers can no longer afford to view the world—an increasingly connected world—through a single cultural lens. Instead, an expanded cultural horizon has become essential to effective leadership. Teams, work groups, communities, and organizations become more diverse every day. Adding new lenses to your cultural viewpoint not only increases your awareness of other cultures and your effectiveness in working with people from other cultures but also develops your understanding of your own cultural conditioning.

There are many personal and leadership benefits of an expanded cultural horizon, and their effects are powerful. You can appreciate different ways—perhaps better ways—of accomplishing goals. You can gain insight into your own behavior. You can discover "out of the box" ways to communicate clearly and effectively. And you can become more comfortable in suspending your judgment, which fosters a more creative work environment.

Cultural differences arise in all levels of an organization and affect all leaders, from the project team to the executive suite. As you become more aware of those differences and more skilled at communicating across cultures, you'll become a better manager and a more effective leader.

Gaining a Critical Edge
in Mastering Globalization

The GROVEWELL-CFGU Partnership

Organizations in the United States have long been putting into practice the ideals of diversity and inclusion. In doing so they have learned that inclusion is not only the right thing to do but also good for the bottom line. As globalization has become a fact of life for today's organizations, the lessons learned in the U.S. pursuit of diversity and inclusion are, to some extent, applicable worldwide. But to apply those lessons effectively, intercultural consulting needs to become involved.

For most large organizations today, globalization is a fact of life. Global operations must be mastered and global market share captured. To accomplish that, good working partnerships must be maintained with people who are as different as they are distant. How can leaders, pressed on all sides, find the resources to enable their organizations to meet the resulting challenges?

The surprising answer is that dedicated resources for building partnerships with customers, suppliers, employees, and other stakeholders abroad have long been at hand. Seasoned experts with practical business experience are readily available from two areas of specialization. One is very well known: diversity and inclusion. The other is not: intercultural consulting.

For many years in the United States and much more recently in Europe, companies and organizations have been putting into practice the ideals of diversity and inclusion. At first the principal motive for this change was that it was the right thing to do. As inclusion became the norm a second motive emerged: inclusion is good for the bottom line.

A major complexity of globalization is that the people one deals with abroad are diverse—more diverse than those one encounters at home. Nevertheless, the lessons learned in pursuing diversity and inclusion at home are, to some extent, applicable worldwide.

But to apply those lessons effectively, the second business-oriented area of expertise—intercultural consulting—needs to become involved. Its contribution is a body of knowledge and practice amassed worldwide. Together, intercultural consulting and diversity and inclusion offer business leaders a critical edge in mastering globalization.

VALUING DIFFERENCE

Practitioners of diversity and inclusion, who until recently have worked almost exclusively in the United States, have been involved in research, consulting, education and training, public advocacy, workplace and community engagement, legal work and legislative lobbying, and above all organizational transformation. Their success is plain to see: today few U.S. organizations offer employees and customers a homogeneous environment.

Instead, conscious efforts are made to value human differences in gender, race and ethnicity, age, and other traits. The resulting expansion of employees' backgrounds and perspectives invigorates a company's efforts to think outside the box and to appeal to the sensitivities of multiple domestic markets. All this effort and experience can be reapplied to globalization.

Indeed, diversity practitioners are turning their attention to globalization. A term heard more and more often since 2000 is *global diversity;* at a minimum it geographically extends the long-established meaning of diversity (and of inclusion).

But that isn't enough. Leaders must begin to understand global diversity in light of a set of facts more complicated—and more promising in terms of global revenue—than most business-people expect.

One complication is that relative to our dom
rience, globalization brings us face to face with m
variation and more types of human variation. Has ͨ
inclusion work so far prepared us for this? Yes and no: yes ͨ
we do have some idea of the challenges ahead, and no because
we're now going to take the diversity concept beyond its original
cultural base. Our new mission is to build and maintain working partnerships with counterparts abroad. So the *global* in *global
diversity* can no longer be limited to meaning *geographically more
inclusive*. It must also mean *culturally aware* and, beyond that,
culturally calibrated in terms of the values and expectations of local
businesspeople.

The term *genuinely global* is useful. A manager, team, or unit
that is genuinely global is vigilant for variations in human values
and practices between one geographical locality and another, and
asks, *To prosper here, what should we be doing differently?*

To find the answer, organizations and individuals can tap
interculturalists' five decades of experience.

CLASHING VALUES

The intercultural field is a branch of the behavioral sciences, with
both academic and consulting wings. The research-based academic
wing generates hundreds of publications each year in the form of
doctoral dissertations, books, and journal articles. Benefiting from
this output is the consulting wing, which delivers to global organizations strategic consulting, executive coaching, global leadership
development, and expatriate performance enhancement.

Intercultural consulting is not as widely known among
business leaders as diversity and inclusion are. The intercultural
field arose during the 1950s out of two themes. A public theme
emerged from the lingering black cloud of World War II and
the Holocaust and the resulting determination to overcome hate
and violence. This theme is well represented in Gordon Allport's
widely praised 1954 book, *The Nature of Prejudice.*

What does intercultural work look like? The researchers study group-level (that is, shared) values, habits of thought, and patterns of behavior—known collectively as *culture*. They provide a welcome counterweight to the Western tendency to seek explanations in individual uniqueness. Their research is practice oriented—it develops methods and tools that enable people to succeed when collaborating with others with whom they lack deep familiarity. The consultants apply the results of this research together with other types of expertise to address performance challenges in the global arena. Intercultural consultants help managers seize global opportunities and attain strategic objectives.

Even those who know of this field aren't always aware of the richness and potential positive impact of intercultural research and services. Consider the Global Leadership and Organizational Behavior Effectiveness (GLOBE) project. Led by the Wharton School of the University of Pennsylvania, this project probed the behaviors of business leaders in sixty-two societies to discover what enabled these leaders to be perceived as highly effective. GLOBE's findings can help a corporation in making its leadership development efforts genuinely global. (A comprehensive overview of GLOBE's findings can be found at www.grovewell.com/GLOBE.)

Globalization is a multifaceted, complex process. One of its critical challenges—the building of good working partnerships with others abroad—can be mastered with the combined support of diversity practitioners and interculturalists. Is there a basis for synergy between these two professions? Let's explore their differences and similarities.

DIVERGING PATHS

There are three key differences between diversity practitioners and intercultural consultants.

An obvious difference is that diversity practitioners have focused primarily on diversity within the United States and U.S. organizations. (Recently, European organizations as well have begun addressing diversity.) But for fifty years the work of inter-culturalists has spanned the globe.

A second difference is that diversity practitioners are heirs to a tradition of in-the-streets activism. They're associated with a tumultuous and celebrated period in recent U.S. history, the stuff of headlines, books, films, songs, petitions, poems, and prayers. Interculturalists continue a research tradition. The Peace Corps' predicament during the 1960s didn't send angry masses into the streets; it sent anthropologists and sociologists into the field and to their desks to figure out what had gone wrong. They and those who followed them have generated insights and applications for improved performance across cultures. Interculturalists are active but they're not activists.

A third difference contrasts political and neutral approaches. The work of diversity practitioners has a political aim. They try to narrow the gap separating core values about respect for others from daily actions in U.S. citizens' lives. They promote a set of behaviors and underlying values as right and good for everyone. Interculturalists also deal with behaviors and underlying values but from a neutral stance. The term for this neutrality is *cultural relativism,* the view that the desirability of any behavior is best determined in relation to the core values of the culture in which it originated. Interculturalists focus on behavior modification for the benefit of an organization or individual, helping businesspeople improve their global competencies.

For an example of cultural relativism, recall the predicament of those early Peace Corps volunteers. Their core value of progress motivated them to suggest a new behavior, building an irrigation system. But for many villagers that behavior clashed with one or more of their society's core values. For instance, some villagers foresaw that irrigation for all could undermine their long-standing structure of hierarchical relationships.

COMMON GROUND

Their differences notwithstanding, these two professions do have something in common. Significantly, both are concerned with values. We have been portraying diversity practitioners as promoting alignment of U.S. citizens' behaviors with a certain set of values, and interculturalists as value-aware but neutral as they enable businesspeople to fine-tune their behaviors for success abroad. A closer look reveals more complexity.

Diversity practitioners employ two perspectives on values: values as imperative and values as relative. The imperative values are a trio of bedrock U.S. values that impel the activism of diversity practitioners and anchor the behaviors with which these practitioners hope to align all citizens. This value trio comprises

Egalitarianism. People should compete on a level playing field as they strive to get ahead; fairness and equal opportunity should prevail in the workplace.

Achievement. People should obtain opportunities and rewards because of their attainments, not because of ascribed traits such as skin color, gender, or age.

Individualism. People should be self-sufficient and self-expressive; supervisors should give every employee the opportunity to apply his or her unique talents.

Diversity practitioners believe that by promoting egalitarianism, achievement, and individualism, they are doing what is right and good. They view this trio of values as a motivating imperative.

A second strong motivator for diversity practitioners has been the gathering chorus of research findings revealing that human diversity—that is, human heterogeneity in working groups—leads to greater innovation, improved problem solving, better customer relations, superior decision making, and other bottom-line benefits for globalizing businesses.

Whether for moral propriety or improved profits or both, diversity practitioners have tended to promote the values of diversity and inclusion as an imperative. Less obvious is the fact that these practitioners work equally with relative values. Diversity practitioners have been leaders in recognizing the worth in every human being and creating workplaces in which everyone feels respected and can contribute his or her perspectives and talents. To accomplish this the practitioners urge people to be accepting of the traditions, mind-sets, and values of fellow employees of every description. In short, they adopt the stance of cultural relativism.

Interculturalists and diversity practitioners therefore share a key approach: cultural relativism. Both groups have worked long and hard to bring about open-mindedness toward, inclusion of, and respectful interactions among people of every description. Both sets of professionals have consistently denied that anyone, anywhere, can justifiably claim, *My values and ways of life are the only ones that are right for all others.* Both groups avow that such a claim is neither ethically defensible nor commercially advantageous.

Cultural relativism is deeply grounded in both professions, a fact that eclipses their superficial differences in style. In our view these professions' previously parallel but rarely intersecting activities can be transformed into synergies and thus into practical advantages for globalizing enterprises.

CHANCES FOR PROGRESS

In addition to their unmet need for guidance and support as they craft collaborative partnerships with counterparts from abroad, many business leaders will need help to

- Generate not only greater market share but also local admiration and loyalty in distant regions.

- Develop globally focused metrics into a cohesive and ultimately systemic model of performance management.

- Facilitate high performance of those indispensable virtual teams (which tend to have poor track records).

- Align and coordinate the worldwide infrastructure that gets day-to-day work done.
- Build a heterogeneous group of globally minded leaders within a worldwide learning culture.

There's much that can be done. Help for business leaders who are determined to get it done is waiting to be harnessed. The key is for organizations to involve both interculturalists and diversity practitioners.

For organizations with diversity professionals on their staff, we suggest asking these professionals to begin by learning more about the intercultural field. This field has a burgeoning literature, most of which is written with practical business needs in mind.

Next, invite interculturalists to meet with the diversity staff. Most interculturalists know about and support diversity and inclusion but do not know how diversity practitioners work in organizations.

Once mutual familiarity has been attained, ask the combined group to explore how your organization could achieve global growth more effectively and how geographical globalization could be increasingly transformed into genuine globalization. In this way the fifty-year-old field of interculturalism can be applied to leverage the in-house experience of your diversity staff to help you master globalization.

If It's *Lagom*, This Must Be Sweden

Kristina Williams and Kay Devine

The characteristic *lagom*—loosely translated as "enough, sufficient, adequate, or just right"—is deeply embedded in Swedish culture and thus in the Swedish leadership style, with its emphasis on egalitarianism and consensus. Certain aspects of the Swedish leadership style, if adopted by leaders elsewhere in the world, might result in beneficial outcomes.

Lagom permeates Swedish culture so thoroughly that many successful Swedish leaders practice it instinctively. Perhaps this is why so many Swedish companies—including Alfa Laval, AGA, Electrolux, Ericsson, IKEA, Volvo, and Scandinavian Airlines—are well-known success stories.

What is *lagom*? According to folklore, it is a contraction of *laget om* ("around the team"), a phrase used by the Vikings to specify how much mead one should drink from the horn as it was passed around, to ensure that everyone would receive a fair share. The Lexin Swedish-English Dictionary defines *lagom* as "enough, sufficient, adequate, or just right," but no direct English equivalent exists. Michael Maccoby, editor of *Sweden at the Edge: Lessons for American and Swedish Managers* (University of Pennsylvania Press, 1991), may have explained it best when he commented in his introduction to the book that "Swedish children learn that putting either too much or too little on the plate is not *lagom,* and Swedish unions demand that wages be *lagom* enough to create solidarity."

Although *lagom* is uniquely Scandinavian, it's only one among a number of characteristics that Western leaders should take into account when working with Swedish companies. It is known that leadership styles vary considerably by culture, as research—such as the Global Leadership and Organizational Behavior Effectiveness Research Program, a multiphase, multi-method project in which investigators around the world are examining the interrelationships between societal culture, organizational culture, and organizational leadership—has determined that the people of Scandinavia have views distinctly different from those of Americans, Asians, Eastern Europeans, Arabs, and others.

The most frequent descriptors of Swedish leadership styles include these concepts: egalitarianism, a high degree of consensus, participative decision making, a focus on teams, and informality of relations between leader and employee. An amalgamation of the two most often used descriptors—egalitarianism and consensus—best portrays *lagom*. This Swedish value of *just enough* can be contrasted with the North American value of *more is better. Lagom* is viewed favorably as an alternative to the extremes of consumerism: "Why do I need more than two? *Det är* ['It is'] *lagom.*"

UNIQUE APPROACH

Ten Swedish leaders from various industries were interviewed and asked about their leadership styles. Of the ten, eight strongly believed that there is a distinct Swedish leadership approach to managing. Sweden is unique in its dual philosophy of individualism and collectivism, a philosophy that provides a basis for team success. In contrast, a purely individualistic emphasis, as often embodied in North American practice, leads to the sacrifice of team goals, whereas a purely collectivist view can lead to mediocrity. A team consists of individuals, and if these individuals do not function effectively, the team also will not function effectively. For example, when measuring results, it doesn't matter if one out of ten individuals reaches or surpasses his or her goals if the other nine underperform. The desired outcome is to raise the performance of each individual on the team so that everyone is working at the same, optimal level. As stated by one Swedish executive: "You have to make the team work because you cannot trade in your players. You have to work with what you have and make sure they produce results."

The Swedish workplace is also distinctive in that most employee-supervisor relationships are informal, and open communication is the norm. It is considered important that employees feel comfortable discussing problems and asking questions. Face-to-face communication is the preferred communication medium, and active listening is an important element in discussions. This runs counter to the North American trend of relying heavily on e-mail and other electronic forms of communication.

Closely linked to the Swedish style of informality in relationships are informality in control and the use of participative decision making. Employees are often consulted in decisions that will affect them personally, even though management makes the final decision. When employees are informed and engaged in the decision-making process, there is more buy-in and commitment to the work. Managers in Sweden trust that once they delegate a task, it will be completed. Furthermore, employees are given autonomy in determining how to complete a task and are expected to contact a superior only if something goes wrong. Although Swedish supervisors, like their North American counterparts, bear ultimate responsibility for work outcomes, their attitudes differ in that they realize supervisors do not always develop the best solutions. One of the strengths of this nondirective style is that employees, through their participation in the decision making and their high degree of autonomy, feel responsible for the organization and will accomplish tasks even if a supervisor is not present.

CONFLICT AND EMOTION

In every work situation there is conflict. Early studies of Swedish leadership styles suggested that managing conflict was generally avoided. Today's Swedish managers, however, report that they prefer to deal with conflict in its nascent stages, when it is only a difference in opinion and not yet a conflict. The prevailing thought is that the longer you wait, the bigger the problem becomes. As one Swedish executive said, it takes twenty-four hours for people to convince themselves that they are right. It's better to discuss problems with people before strong positions are taken.

Although emotional quotient, or EQ, has become acknowledged worldwide as an important leadership attribute, Swedish culture remains uncomfortable with overt emotional displays. Paradoxically, despite their unemotional countenance, Swedish executives are likely to exhibit a people-oriented leadership style. They are considered caring and supportive, and they rank employees as the most important factor influencing productivity. Other examples of this caring nature are exhibited in executives' desire to understand their employees' problems and in the country's legal and social frameworks, such as provisions for extended paternity leave for fathers and a mandatory five weeks of vacation. Swedish leaders believe that without creative, hardworking employees, even the best leadership style will fail.

In addition, most Swedish leaders do not view themselves as superior to their employees. Typically, no formal trappings of leadership such as titles are used, and communication occurs on a first-name basis. As one Swedish executive commented, one does not gain respect by position or title but rather by one's actions. In other words, leadership is not positional—it is earned.

Without a doubt, Swedish executives believe in their style of management. Their beliefs are supported by research. According to *Sweden at the Edge,* companies that incorporate participation and cooperation into their management philosophy report positive results. However, this leadership style that works so well in Sweden could be problematic for North American organizations that attempt to implement it. The reason is differences in employee expectations. In Sweden, employees expect and may even demand to be consulted, whereas North American employees assume that their supervisors will make decisions without consulting them. In Sweden, employees question decisions, whereas in North America employees do as they are told without questions. So it would be difficult to adopt the complete concept of the Swedish leadership style in North America.

Globalization has had some effect on the Swedish leadership style. Swedish companies that have many non-Swedish employees tend to shy away from consensus, one of the key descriptors of the Swedish leadership style. Today's Swedish executives say that now it is important only that the employees who enact a decision agree with it. When international employees are involved in a project, they may not be consulted at all. Overall, however, the Swedish style of leadership has maintained its distinctiveness and has not experienced major change.

There are certain characteristics of the Swedish leadership style that if implemented by leaders elsewhere in the world might result in beneficial outcomes. As Swedish leaders would advise, however, *lagom* must be practiced when adopting the styles of others.

Seeking a Model for Leadership Development in China

Elizabeth Weldon

The author's research has revealed some preliminary conclusions about Chinese leadership and how it differs from leadership in North America, attitudes toward leadership development in Chinese firms, and Chinese managers' desire to participate in the same type of developmental experiences used in the West, such as 360-degree feedback and coaching. The results suggest that Western practices such as CCL's approach to development (assessment, challenge, and support) may be good models for China.

Western companies continue to invest in China, with many companies integrating their Chinese operations into their global strategies. These organizations, along with Chinese companies—whether private or state-owned—all need more-effective leaders.

The manager of a state-owned enterprise (SOE) in China recently approached me hoping to find a competency model designed specifically for China to guide leadership development in his company. A competency model defines the skills, characteristics, and behavior of an effective leader.

Inspired by this and by the debate about the differences between Western and Chinese leadership, I did some preliminary research using a North American model of leadership developed by James Kouzes and Barry Posner, coauthors of the best-selling book *The Leadership Challenge: How to Make Extraordinary Things Happen in Organizations* (Jossey-Bass, 2012, fifth edition). From their descriptions of exemplary leadership, I generated a list of leadership behaviors and asked 103 midlevel and senior Chinese managers to indicate how important each behavior is to effective leadership in their companies.

The results of this survey allow three preliminary conclusions about Chinese leadership and how it differs from leadership in North America. First, building strong bonds based on collaboration, teamwork, dignity, and trust is a key element of both Chinese and North American leadership. Second, like North American leaders, leaders in China believe that one of their main roles is to improve the company; North American leaders, however, place more value on experimentation and taking risks. Finally, although Chinese leaders believe it is important to help others succeed, they also believe that this is of secondary importance. This finding departs from Kouzes and Posner's model and from the beliefs of many North American business leaders, who say that today's leaders must be coaches, facilitators, and helpmates to enable others to succeed.

In another survey I looked at attitudes toward leadership development in Chinese firms. I pursued this issue with a questionnaire to 172 senior executives and top functional managers working in SOEs, foreign-invested enterprises, and private Chinese firms.

Overall, 51 percent strongly agreed that developing people was one of their company's top three objectives. However, only 15 percent felt strongly that the managers in their company knew how to do this efficiently and effectively.

This illuminates three important points. First, although managers believe that developing the people they lead is important, most of them don't know how to do it. Second, all managers must learn how to develop their people. And third, once managers have the skills needed to develop their people, they should be held accountable for accomplishing this task.

In a third short survey I found that senior Chinese managers would like to participate in the same types of developmental experiences used in the West, such as 360-degree feedback and coaching. These Chinese managers also want to be challenged and believe they can learn from challenge.

This last point was borne out by another survey I did of young, high-potential Chinese managers. Overall, the results showed that managers who are allowed to take on new responsibilities and tackle new tasks in their daily work are more satisfied with their opportunities to develop than are those who are not given such responsibilities and tasks.

It would appear therefore that Western practices such as CCL's approach to development (assessment, challenge, and support) are good models for China. Working with local experts should help us tailor the models to the Chinese context.

ABOUT THE CONTRIBUTORS

Shannon Cranford is manager of custom operations at CCL in Greensboro, North Carolina. Her responsibilities include managing Greensboro's custom program project managers, who are responsible for leading the planning and execution of customized initiatives for CCL clients.

Craig Chappelow is global assessment portfolio manager at CCL in Greensboro, North Carolina, where he manages CCL's suite of 360-degree assessment instruments.

Maxine A. Dalton worked at CCL for fourteen years. She managed, trained, and developed materials for the Tools for Developing Successful Executives Program. She is now retired and lives in Spring Creek, North Carolina.

David V. Day is Winthrop Professor and Woodside Chair of Leadership and Management at the University of Western Australia.

Jennifer J. Deal is a senior research scientist at CCL's San Diego campus.

Kay Devine is an associate professor of organizational behavior and analysis at Athabasca University in Alberta, Canada.

Christopher Ernst is organizational effectiveness thought leader at Juniper Networks in California's Silicon Valley. Previously he was research director of global leadership at CCL's Singapore campus and, prior to that, a research associate at CCL in Greensboro, North Carolina. He is a coauthor of *Boundary Spanning Leadership: Six Practices for Solving Problems, Driving Innovation, and Transforming Organizations* (McGraw-Hill Professional, 2011).

Sarah Glover is community impact manager, income and resources, at United Way of Greater Greensboro, North Carolina. Previously she was a research analyst in the Research, Innovation, and Product Development Group at CCL in Greensboro.

Michael H. Hoppe is owner of Michael H. Hoppe Consulting, LLC, in Chapel Hill, North Carolina and an adjunct executive coach at CCL. Previously he was a senior faculty member at CCL in Greensboro, North Carolina.

Andrew P. Kakabadse is a professor of international management development at the Cranfield School of Management in the United Kingdom.

Sam Lam is president of Linkage Asia, a leadership development and organizational development consultancy.

Jean Brittain Leslie is a senior fellow and director of applied research services at CCL in Greensboro, North Carolina.

Ancella Livers is a senior faculty member at CCL in Greensboro, North Carolina.

Mohit Misra is vice president and global head of talent management and organizational development for oncology at Novartis Pharmaceuticals.

Patricia M. G. O'Connor is general manager of leadership development and talent management at Wesfarmers Ltd. in Perth, Australia. Previously she was research director, emerging leadership practices, at CCL's Singapore campus.

Don W. Prince is general manager of CCL's office in Moscow.

Hal Richman worked with the U.N. Development Program for seven years and is currently doing consulting work on developing organizational capacity to manage learning and performance.

Joo-Seng Tan is an associate professor of management at Nanyang Technological University's Nanyang School of Business in Singapore.

The GROVEWELL-CFGU Partnership is an alliance between GROVEWELL, LLC, a firm that delivers strategic consulting and executive coaching worldwide, and the Consortium for Global Understanding (CFGU), which delivers large-scale diversity and inclusion services worldwide. "Gaining a Critical Edge in Mastering Globalization" in this volume was written by four members of the partnership: Cornelius N. Grove, founder and a partner at GROVEWELL; Willa Zakin Hallowell, a partner at GROVEWELL; Kathy Molloy, a senior associate at GROVEWELL; and Shannon Murphy Robinson, founder and managing director of CFGU.

Elizabeth Weldon is a professor of management at Pennsylvania State University's Smeal College of Business. She was the H. Smith Richardson Jr. Visiting Fellow at CCL in 2004.

A. William Wiggenhorn is a former longtime president of Motorola University and is currently a principal at Main Captiva, LLC, where he is responsible for custom-designed executive development strategy, systems, and programs as well as talent management strategies and systems.

Kristina Williams is director of investments at Alberta Enterprise, which invests in venture capital funds that finance technology startups in Alberta, Canada.

Jeffrey Yip is a lecturer in organizational management and doctoral candidate at Boston University School of Management and a visiting researcher at CCL. Previously he was a research associate at CCL's Singapore campus.

FURTHER READING

(2003). *Executive reader: Insights on leadership and development.* Greensboro, NC: Center for Creative Leadership.

Dalton, M. A., & Ernst, C. T. (2004). Developing leaders for global roles. In C. D. McCauley & E. Van Velsor (Eds.), *The Center for Creative Leadership handbook of leadership development,* 2nd ed. (pp. 361–382). San Francisco, CA: Jossey-Bass and Center for Creative Leadership.

Dalton, M. A., Ernst, C. T., Deal, J. J., & Leslie, J. B. (2002). *Success for the new global manager: What you need to know to work across distances, countries, and cultures.* San Francisco, CA: Jossey-Bass and Center for Creative Leadership.

Leslie, J. B., & Van Velsor, E. (1998). *A cross-national comparison of effective leadership and teamwork: Toward a global workforce.* Greensboro, NC: Center for Creative Leadership.

Leslie, J. B., Dalton, M., Ernst, C., & Deal, J. (2002). *Managerial effectiveness in a global context.* Greensboro, NC: Center for Creative Leadership.

McCauley, C. D., & Van Velsor, E. (2004). *The Center for Creative Leadership handbook of leadership development* (2nd ed.). San Francisco, CA: Jossey-Bass and Center for Creative Leadership.

Wilcox, M., & Rush, S. (Eds.). (2004). *The CCL guide to leadership in action: How managers and organizations can improve the practice of leadership.* San Francisco, CA: Jossey-Bass and Center for Creative Leadership.

Wilson, M. S., & Dalton, M. A. (1998). *International success: Selecting, developing, and supporting expatriate managers.* Greensboro, NC: Center for Creative Leadership.

Ordering Information

To get more information, to order other CCL Press publications, or to find out about bulk-order discounts, please contact us by phone at 336-545-2810 or visit our online bookstore at www.ccl.org/publications.

CPSIA information can be obtained at www.ICGtesting.com
Printed in the USA
BVOW01s1030240913

331692BV00004B/14/P